The GURS HAGGADAH
PASSOVER IN PERDITION

Bella Gutterman and Naomi Morgenstern

The Gurs Haggadah: Passover in Perdition

Published by Devora Publishing and Yad Vashem

Translation: Nechama Kanner
Editing: Yaacov Peterseil

Cover Design and Book Design by Benjie Herskowitz

Translated from *Passover Haggadah from The Gurs Camp, France, 1941* with permission from Yad Vashem, Jerusalem, Israel
Web site: www.yadvashem.org

Photograph Research: Nina Springer-Aharoni

Photographs: Yad Vashem Archive
Gurs Camp Museum Archive
Central City Archive, Stuttgart
Private Collection, Oskar Althausen, Mannheim

Illustrations: Art Museum Collection, Yad Vashem

Cover photo supplied by Dani Karavan

E-mail: pitspop@netvision.net.il Web site: www.devorapublishing.com

ISBN: 1-930143-33-8

Printed in Israel

This book is dedicated
to the memory of all those
who were imprisoned
at the Gurs camp,
and found the inner strength to continue
with the wellspring
of religious and cultural creativity.

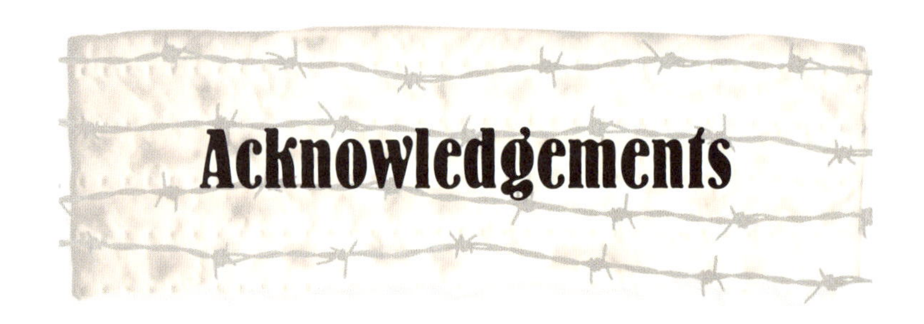

Many people contributed to the production of this book.

Much gratitude and appreciation to Rabbi A. Yehoshu'a Zuckerman, the son of the author of the Gurs Haggadah, for his willingness to share his reflections.

Commendations to Dr. Pinhas Rothschild, Mr. Oskar Althausen, Dr. Ehud Loeb, Mr. Max Ansbacher, and Mr. Yizhak Kremer, former inmates of the Gurs camp.

Dr. Pinhas Rothschild, with his phenomenal memory, shared with us significant and rare details about the camp. Oskar Althausen, chairman of the Mannheim Christian-Jewish Friendship Association, gave us testimonies and photographs, and was willing, from afar, to honor our every request. Dr. Ehud Loeb, one of the children of the Gurs camp, assisted us throughout the project by gathering information, translating, and establishing contacts. Yizhak Kremer allowed us the use of his memoirs from the camp.

Special thanks:

To Yehudit Rotem who, within a short time, organized a great deal of material and prepared the groundwork for this publication.

To Mr. Dani Karavan, for allowing us use of the monument which he designed at Gurs.

To Mr. Sha'ul Oren and the volunteers at the museum, Erma Sharon, Yonah Shilgi, Ruth Mittleman, Shulamit Hakenbruch, Miriam Doron and Graciella Martinotti who helped translate the texts.

To museum staff members Osnat Sirkin and Sharon Yuzer, and to Yonah Gal and Dorit Re'uven from the International School for Holocaust Studies.

Thank you to Bracha Freundlich for her assistance in acquiring important sources.

Thanks to Mr. Arnon Magen for his translations from the German.

Contents

EIN·FRÜHLING
LÖW+
BODEK

The Passover Haggadah from the Gurs Camp

The archives at Yad Vashem include rare, moving materials from which various items are chosen for their monthly "Special Exhibits Display Case." The Passover Haggadah from Gurs, which was written in the Gurs detention camp in southwestern France, was exhibited during Passover 5758/1998. The Haggadah attracted much attention and provoked great interest among visitors, many of whom inquired about the details surrounding its compilation during the Holocaust.

The Gurs Haggadah was handwritten under difficult conditions in preparation for Passover 5701/1941, and was distributed among camp inmates who used it to conduct a *Seder* according to *halakha* (religious law). Its compilation under these circumstances and the care taken in observing the holiday reflect the traditional/religious aspect that characterized, in part, the fabric of Jewish life in the camps and ghettos.

The Gurs camp was one of several detention camps to which recent immigrants to France – Jews and others – were taken after the outbreak of the Second World War. These were joined by thousands of Jews who were deported from Belgium and Germany in October 1940.

The lives of the Jewish prisoners were unbearably difficult, with disease and death their constant companions. Nevertheless, the prisoners never refrained from helping one another, loving their fellow man, and pursuing spiritual creativity. Behind the barbed wire fences, the inmates established a wonderful world filled with imagination and beauty, in stark contrast to the camp's barren and muddy surroundings. Rabbis and spiritual leaders organized religious life and provided solace to those in need.

This book presents the story of the Jews imprisoned in the Gurs camp. It reveals the strength of the human spirit which, even when locked behind barbed wire, can continue to create a world of hope and light.

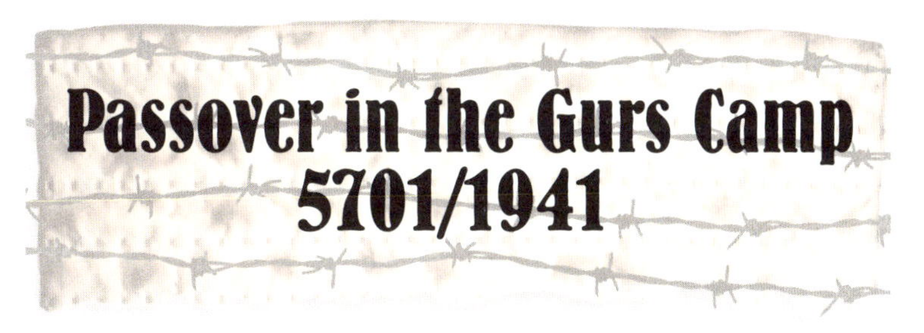

Passover in the Gurs Camp 5701/1941

Pinhas Rothschild

At the time, celebrating the Passover holiday in the Gurs camp, we felt as if a refreshing breeze from the Promised Land had descended upon us via the desert: "By the strength of His hand, God took us out from the house of slavery."

Before Gurs, we had led a carefree existence in the Diaspora, and had not attempted to truly understand or remember the miracle of the Exodus from Egypt – from slavery to freedom. Now, it was as if that which befell our nation in those distant days touched us and became part of our everyday existence. Then as now: the reality and the expectations. We vacillated between the hope for freedom and the hardships still waiting for us, as we began to prepare for the holiday week in the camp.

The most difficult Passover problem was already solved. Even though many supplies were missing, we were able to obtain matzot – as in all the years since the Exodus from Egypt. Notices hung by the local Rabbinate, as well as the sermon of the rabbi on the Sabbath before Passover, made us aware of what was permitted or forbidden. An unknown source, as if by Divine Providence, provided new cooking and eating utensils. Silently, and in an orderly fashion, the men sat in their barracks and the women in theirs, scouring plates, pots, forks, and spoons. Wood ash was used to give the utensils a final polish before they were made kosher for the holiday.

The Central Assistance Committee members went around the barracks collecting money for the holiday meal. Not everyone could contribute, because during the course of the long months, many had been left penniless. Nevertheless, the table was set for all who were hungry.

The meager Seder tables set for families and groups of friends were prepared with a tremendous outpouring of love mixed with sadness, and were, perhaps, more festive than the large tables in the communal quarters. These tables were covered with the main building material of the camp – tin from empty cans of preserves. Plates and serving trays glistened with the luster of covers and cans. Candles burned in artistically designed candlesticks made of "Gurs metal," their light flickering above the wooden beams of the barracks, reflecting the troubled faces of the people, and their eyes filled with hope and subdued joy. Only the too-few Seder plates were conspicuous against the white paper that covered the wooden tables. Every Seder plate was divided into three parts, fulfilling the commandment of the Seder, and these were covered with lace handkerchiefs and colorful shawls which, one could tell, had been hastily packed in the frenzy of flight.

But the most precious items – more precious in our eyes than all the illustrated and decorated Haggadot which we had once used – were those simple, handwritten Haggadot. After the holiday, these Haggadot became a memory-filled and meticulously guarded possession.

At nightfall, the festive evening commenced with the arrival of the men – husbands, brothers, sons – at the women's barracks, and the night air soon reverberated with the ancient melody of *"Ha lachma anya . . ."*

It would be hard to imagine a more meager Seder meal than was served that evening. In addition to matzah, many were given a little salad in place of the bitter herbs, *haroset,* and an egg. Only a few benefited from a real meal, albeit with tiny portions. Some were lucky enough to receive food packages, which they distributed fairly among the participants.

The April evening, with its refreshing, moisture-filled spring air spread through the dark paths of the camp. Lights penetrated from inside the barracks and the sounds of songs and the Grace After Meals were heard outside. Words which had been sung countless times before, were sung that night with raised spirits, filled with compassion and promise.

"Had Gadya Had Gadya" – thus were the Israelites' tents spread three thousand years ago. Beneath the star-studded sky, in the quiet moonlight, then as today, the Israelites girded their loins – then as now....

The holiday meals were far from lavish, but they were tasty and almost satisfying. Just as the first day of the holiday is holy, so is the last. On that day, thousands of people stood in the square under clear skies. The mountains seemed incredibly close and the snow on the peaks and slopes was as though etched upon them. It seemed as if the raised platform, decorated with lilac shrubs, was lifted to the heavens. The *Magen David* (Star of David) shone and the voice of the prayer leader, who prayed with such feeling, carried over and above the spring-like sounds of the songbirds in the nearby forest. The thousands of persecuted refugees answered *amen*, moved as they were by the words of our holy Torah. Chief Cantor Enoch chanted the *Kaddish* prayer, and the masses, wrapped in a deep, silent sorrow, trembled as he prayed. Rabbi Leo Ansbacher spoke stirringly to the assembled about the dead and the living in the camp – the dead, buried in the nearby cemetery, and the living, those continuing their wandering. With a heart overflowing with hope, the rabbi painted visions of tranquility and a future filled with joy and security, of renewal and fellowship. His words, spoken in German and in the vernacular, brought consolaton. Then a melody from Psalms floated above the people and Chief Cantor Tolman sang the *El Maleh Rahamim*. His deep voice accompanied the return of the Torah to the Holy Ark with the prayer *"Hashivenu Hashem Elekha VeNashuva...."*

Thus, Passover was but a brief respite from the fleeing and wandering, yet closer than previous Passovers to the ancient-new prayer: "Next Year in Jerusalem."

Written after Passover 5701/1941

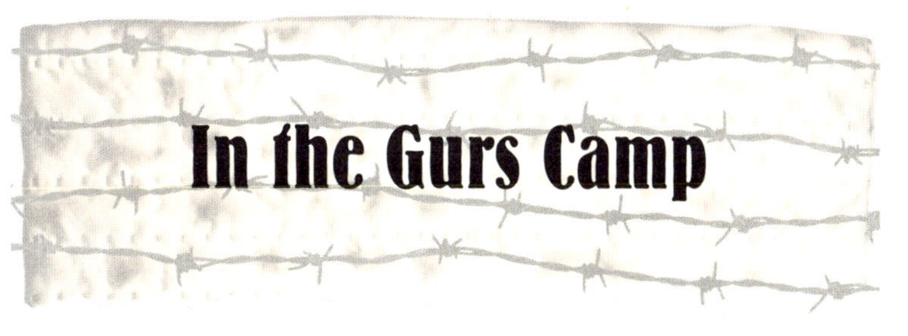

In the Gurs Camp

Bella Gutterman and Naomi Morgenstern

My last fifty-eight years seem shorter to me than my first seven years. A yawning abyss separates these two unequal periods:

Everything changed at Gurs – because of Gurs, right after Gurs, since Gurs. My grandmother died there, my parents were led from Gurs to their deaths in Auschwitz, and my childhood died at Gurs when I was seven years old. It was impossible to revive it.

Ehud Loeb

The Gurs camp was not a death camp; nevertheless, many died there from starvation and disease. It was not a labor camp; yet men who were imprisoned there were sent to hard labor, and its thousands of prisoners never found a moment of peace there. Gurs was a detention camp.

People of all ages – from infancy through advanced old age – were incarcerated there, ostensibly for holding unconventional ideas, but primarily because they were Jews. Many of those who survived the cold and the hunger, the disease and the despair at Gurs, were sent to their deaths in the extermination camps without leaving behind any monument.

A visitor to Gurs today would find few remnants of what happened there.

The camp was totally uprooted and only the two-kilometer asphalt road that divided it remains intact.

At the camp's entrance stands a memorial that was erected in 1944 at the survivors' initiative.

The other eternal monument is the cemetery, where over one thousand people, most of them Jews, are buried.

The Establishment of the Camp

The Gurs camp was established in April 1939 in southwestern France, eighty kilometers from the Spanish border. Gurs was a detention camp and its first prisoners were Republican soldiers who fled to France after the collapse of the Spanish Republic and General Franco's victory.

With the German invasion of Poland in September 1939, and the French-British declaration of war on Germany, France began to hunt German and Austrian subjects, including anti-Nazi activists and Jews who had found refuge in France. In late November 1939 those arrested were transferred to detention camps in southwestern France, the largest of which was Gurs. Thousands of people – men, women, and children – were imprisoned in the camp, and it became necessary to hastily build makeshift shower facilities, as well as latrines and barracks for mothers and young children.

The German attack on France in May 1940 led to another wave of arrests of foreign subjects, mostly Jews, who were sent to Gurs. On June 22, 1940, a cease-fire agreement was signed dividing France into occupied territory, with its capital in Paris, and unoccupied territory, centered in Vichy. Gurs was under Vichy control and all the non-Jewish Germans, the pro-Nazis, and the Communists were released. At the end of 1940 three thousand people remained at the camp, including 980 Jewish women.

Lisa P., a Jewess from Berlin, was active in anti-Fascist circles in Germany, and fled to France with her husband, Hans, in 1933. Lisa was arrested in Paris and sent to the Gurs camp with the other prisoners.

"Get into the barracks!" screamed the woman in charge. The women were divided into groups and were herded into a line of identical huts. Each hut was divided down its length by a long, narrow aisle. Straw-filled mattresses lined both sides, one next to another, with almost no space between them. Lisa went to the far end of the barrack, where an empty corner caught her eye. That seemed preferable to her because it afforded her more space and she would be able to push her back up against the wall. It was difficult to distinguish individuals in the dim light of the bulb that flickered in the center of the ceiling, and the faces of those lying on the mats were blurry.

"Something is poking me," cried one of the women, jumping up from her place that first evening. She stuck her hand inside the mattress and pulled out a piece of paper with some sentences scribbled on it. "Young lady," she read, "I don't know you, but I am the one who prepared this mattress for you and thought of you as I filled it with straw. Amadeo, Spanish Freedom Fighter."

One day, relates Lisa, truckloads of new refugees and immigrants arrived at the camp. Included in the group were sixteen-year old Gisella and her mother. Gisella never laughed or cried. She didn't talk much, but did tell Lisa that her father was beaten to death by Nazis before her eyes, her brother was killed as a volunteer in the anti-Fascist war in Spain, and her mother was all she had. On sunny mornings, Gisella would carefully spread a wool blanket outside and bring her sick mother there to rest. She would sit by her side, gently stroke her, and speak and sing softly into her ear. Ten days later her mother died. Gisella's eyes remained dry.

The Deportations to Gurs

Rabbi Yehudah Leo Ansbacher, who was later appointed camp rabbi, spoke about the deportation of German and Austrian subjects from Belgium to the detention camps in France:

"On Friday, May 10, 1940, while German planes bombed Belgium, I was held for inspection in Brussels, along with other male foreign subjects. We waited in line to have our identity papers checked by clerks who were sitting behind tables set up on the street.

Osias Hofstatter
Gurs Camp, 1941, 1953

Oil on canvas, 61x 88 cm
Collection of
Yad Vashem Art Museum

"On Shabbat I was kept in the school building, along with a large group of German citizens. The fact that I had left Germany seven years earlier out of fear of the Nazis, and had immigrated to Belgium, did not matter one iota. To the Belgians, I and those like me were collaborating with Hitler's army.

"Two days later we were taken to the train station and put on two freight trains which had flags with the words "Fifth Column" flying above them. The trains

traveled southward, and near the French border we were allowed to get out. We stood in two long lines and were given some soup-like liquid from two large vats. There were about forty observant Jews near me who wanted to know if I, the rabbi, thought the soup was kosher. I dipped one finger into the soup, licked off another and declared it 'kosher!' Later I realized that I had been correct in doing so, for immediately after eating we were returned to the trains and traveled for ninety straight hours without stopping, a difficult journey during which several passengers died.

"The train stopped and we were taken off to a grassy area. It was *erev Shabbat*, Friday evening. We gathered for *kabbalat Shabbat* (welcoming the Shabbat prayers), after which I delivered a speech in order to raise morale. We were put on trains again and sent across the border to the French town of Oloron Saint Marie, which was close to the Saint Cyprien concentration camp. When we were taken off the trains and transferred to the trucks that would transport us to the camp, we were surrounded by local residents who shouted 'Death!' and threw all kinds of objects on us.

"There were approximately seven thousand of us who arrived at Saint Cyprien, mostly Jews and a few Germans. In October 1940, after five months in extremely difficult living and sanitary conditions, we were transferred to the Gurs camp. We joined the prisoners, almost all of whom were Jews with foreign citizenship living in France, and German Jews who had been deported during *Succot* 5701 (October 1940) from Baden-Pfaltz to Gurs."

On October 22, 1940 an order was issued to deport the Jews from the Baden, Pfaltz, and Saarland regions of Germany in an operation known as the "Burckel Action." Local Nazi activists initiated this deportation and received support from higher authorities. An arrangement between the German and Vichy governments allowed the Jews to be transported to France. This deportation applied to Jews of all ages, from infants to those age ninety and above.

That very evening Hitler was notified that the Baden district was *Judenrein* – free of Jews.

Reinhard Heydrich, chief of the security police and SS security service and one of the key figures in the design and execution of the Nazis' anti-Jewish policies, wrote about this deportation as follows: "The deportation of the Jews was conducted throughout Baden and Pfaltz without incident. The general population was hardly aware of the operation. Heads of relevant authorities will deal with seizure of Jewish property, its disposition and utilization. Jews in mixed marriages were not deported."

Adele K., a Jewess born in Berlin, living in Karlsruhe, and the widow of a well-to-do Protestant lawyer, was also deported together with her elderly mother.

Osias Hofstatter
Deportation from Brussels, 1940, 1953

Gouache, ink on paper, 27 x 21.5 cm
Collection of Yad Vashem Art Museum
Donated by Dr. Pinhas Rothschild

"They told us that we had to leave within a half hour and could only take one hundred marks and one suitcase per person; the rest of the cash was to be put on the table. Afterwards they left the house, leaving a military policeman to oversee our actions. He was kind-hearted and expressed sympathy for our fate, but was helpless to do anything. I was upset and confused. I had to physically support my elderly mother who had difficulty walking because of a torn tendon, and I had to carry the suitcases which, in my confusion, I had hastily filled, taking the basic necessities I could think of. "At exactly 3:30 the Gestapo reappeared. We were taken into a waiting police car like common criminals and driven away, never to return, while people stared blankly at us. When we arrived at the station, we were pushed into a crowd of people. Near me, a woman was dying and the Gestapo guards shouted, 'Take her! Take her! She's one of yours.' The woman was dragged onto the train where I hope she met a quick death. We waited for three hours and when the train finally started to move westward, I called out: 'Thank God, not to Poland.'"

"They told us that within a half hour they would remove us from the apartment and that each of us could take one suitcase," relates Yitzhak K., who was fourteen years old when he was banished from his home in Mannheim. "No one answered our question about where they were taking us. The junior officer guarding us permitted me to buy some things at the nearby grocery store, and, together with the other Jewish families of our neighborhood, we were gathered in the schoolyard. We were taken by military trucks to large buildings in the adjoining town, Waldhofen, where, lying on the floor in assembly halls, we awaited for morning light. Loud-speakers instructed us to label our suitcases and leave them in place, and then to get onto trucks which took us to the train station. SS soldiers stationed all along the train ordered us to board the waiting cars. As soon as we boarded, we were asked to volunteer to transfer the suitcases to separate cars. My father and some other men volunteered at once, but the SS soldiers felt that the transfer of the suitcases was not proceeding fast enough, so they called for additional volunteers. That is when I first witnessed the cruelty of the SS men. They entered the cars, grabbed some men, threw them onto the platform and

kicked them until they bled.

"We heard announcements forbidding us to open the doors or look outside, and the train started moving, packed with families – the old, the sick, the children – towards the unknown."

The Journey

Yitzhak K. continues his description of the deportation to Gurs. His father, a frequent business traveler, noticed that the train was bound for France, and for a moment they became hopeful that salvation awaited them there.

"There was no lighting in the train and at night we tried to fall asleep sitting up. Suddenly, in the middle of the night, the train came to a halt and an announcement was heard that anyone who moved out of place would be shot on the spot. Several SS soldiers boarded the train and shone bright flashlights into the eyes of the frightened people. They began randomly beating people, shouting, demanding to know where the money they thought we had was hidden. The women and children began to cry and after some terrifying moments, the soldiers left the car and everyone remained seated in the dark....

"At dawn we noticed that the loudspeakers were silent and that the SS car, which had been equipped with machine guns, was gone. We understood that we had crossed the border between occupied and unoccupied France, and we were happy to finally be out of Nazi hands."

On October 24th, after traveling for two consecutive days, the train carrying Yitzhak's family and the Jews of Mannheim stopped in Oloron near the Gurs camp. At the same time, the rest of the Jews from Baden-Pfaltz arrived in other trains.

The deportation of the Baden-Pfaltz Jews took the French authorities by surprise, as they were given no prior notice regarding the transfer of nine trains to the unoccupied zone. There was, therefore, not enough time to make appropriate living arrangements for the deportees.

"In the dark, in pouring rain, we were ordered to get off the trains. Weakened, exhausted, and confused from the grueling trip, we were transferred to open trucks which took us to the Gurs camp. The barricade was opened and we drove up a main road in an area enclosed with a double barbed wire fence. The men were ordered off the trucks, and the women were driven onward. Through a small gate, where a French policeman stood watch, we were pushed into an area surrounded by barbed wire in which stood empty, broken-down wooden huts. We searched in the dark for protection from the downpour and sat down in a dry corner. At dawn, we realized our true situation: we were in an enclosed area, surrounded by a sharp, double barbed wire fence; a large number of the wooden barracks were without floor and ceiling; and people were tramping in the mud that was all around. There were no decent bathroom facilities and people were forced to go outside in the wind and the rain, and use barrels."

Sigismond Kolos-Vari
Deportees

Ink on paper, 21 x 27 cm
Collection of Yad Vashem
Art Museum
Donated by
Dr. Pinhas Rothschild

In the Camp

The snow-capped mountains of the lower Pyrenees rose up a short distance away from the camp. The entrance to the camp was blocked by a movable barricade guarded by police; nearby, on the left, were the supply huts and the camp headquarters. The camp occupied an area two-and-a-half kilometers long and half a kilometer wide, and was surrounded by double barbed wire fences. An asphalt road ran down the center of the camp with rows of barracks – mostly dilapidated – squeezed together on either side. Each barrack could house up to sixty people under very crowded conditions; each group of twenty-five barracks formed a block, marked with a Latin letter. There were thirteen such blocks, each surrounded by an additional barbed wire fence with guards posted at the entrance. Separate men and women's quarters were in blocks on either side of the road; older children lived with the parent of the same gender. Couples were forbidden to meet for weeks on end and the accompanying loneliness was constant and painful. There were no trees or bushes, grass or greenery in sight – only deep, oozing mud.

Dr. Yitzhak Eugene Neter, a pediatrician, was head of the Jewish community in Mannheim. When the Jews of Mannheim were ordered to leave their homes, Dr. Neter was told that he would be permitted to remain in his house. Nevertheless, Dr. Neter opted to join his community and parted from his wife, who stayed in the city. Their only son had left Germany immediately after the Nazis' rise to power, and settled in Israel where he moved to Kibbutz Degania in the Jordan Valley. This is how Dr. Neter described the Gurs camp:

"It is impossible to put into words what the ground of the camp looked like. Whoever was not there during the initial months, especially during the rainy season, cannot imagine the horror. Every time we left the barracks we would sink up to our ankles, and often even deeper, into the softened earth. I would often find myself at the same place that some poor soul had to be lifted up after getting stuck in the swampy, slimy mud. As soon as we stepped off the only solid dirt path in the camp, our struggle with the mud would begin. Our light shoes, especially the women's, were no match for this untamed bog. The muck penetrated the shoes and our feet were continuously damp."

Ehud L., an only son, was sent to the Gurs camp with his parents, grandmother, and the rest of the Jews from the town of Bühl in Baden:

"I was six-and-a-half years old and helped build the stone paths in the oozing mud. I remember each stone that we found and put in place – I, my mother, and the women who lived with us in the cold, wet barracks.

"I did not see my father from the moment I arrived in Gurs. He was in the men's section. Everything was gray and cold. The rain never ceased and I was forced to sleep on a pile of wet straw which served as a bed. Mother obtained a little wool and knitted a pair of gloves that she exchanged for small amounts of milk for me.

"From the first day at Gurs, I did not stop missing Mother and Father's bed. At Gurs I began to realize that my life had become more than I could bear, a living hell."

Rafi P., age 14, was separated from his mother and, together with his father, was assigned to one of the men's blocks. Rafi describes the makeshift kitchen and the sub-standard food that was prepared at the camp:

"There was an improvised kitchen in a shed where huge dishes were heated on a coal fire. People lacked eating utensils, not having brought them from home. We therefore fashioned something out of tin cans, making handles out of barbed wire we had dismantled, using these makeshift utensils for eating the food distributed to us three times a day. In the morning we received a piece of bread and a brownish liquid which passed for coffee. The midday and evening fare consisted of a thin, watery soup containing a few beans, which remained hard even after twenty-four hours of cooking. Three times a week, a few lucky people found a piece of meat in their soup. This, together with approximately 250 grams of bread, was what we ate every day."

Rabbi Ansbacher also confirms that "the food at Gurs was so wretched that many people died of malnutrition. I remember having the same menu for three-four months. On Sundays or their Easter or, on the other hand, one of our holidays, they brought something else. But usually every lunch and supper we ate the same food that had the same color that had the same taste. For example, during the course of about four months we had kielbasa twice a day, every day."

People, particularly the elderly and the infirm, fell sick, one after another. Dysentery claimed victims very quickly, because although there was no shortage of prisoner-doctors who worked from morning till night, there were no medicines available with which to save people. They were helpless in the face of the plague. Around nine hundred people, among them Yitzhak K.'s and Ehud L.'s grandmothers, died during the first weeks after their arrival at the camp.

In his memoirs, Dr. Neter devoted much space to the poor state of health among the camp's inmates:

"The results of the terrible health conditions were most tragic. In November-December 1940 we witnessed mass deaths. An intestinal epidemic spread through the camp. The adjustment to their new, difficult life so weakened the people – particularly the many elderly – that both physically and emotionally their will to resist was broken. The doctors and nurses struggled in vain to provide relief. Drug supplies were overwhelmingly scarce, the shortage of linen caused terrible filth, and most unbearable was the physical and emotional suffering that resulted. Over six hundred men and women perished in those three months. Their hearts, their entire bodies were unable to withstand such a traumatic change of life, and they succumbed. Thus was the will to live crushed under these unbearable surroundings."

"My mother and I were taken to what was referred to as the clinic, something that resembled a hut for the sick, and we were given hot food," recalls Adele K. of

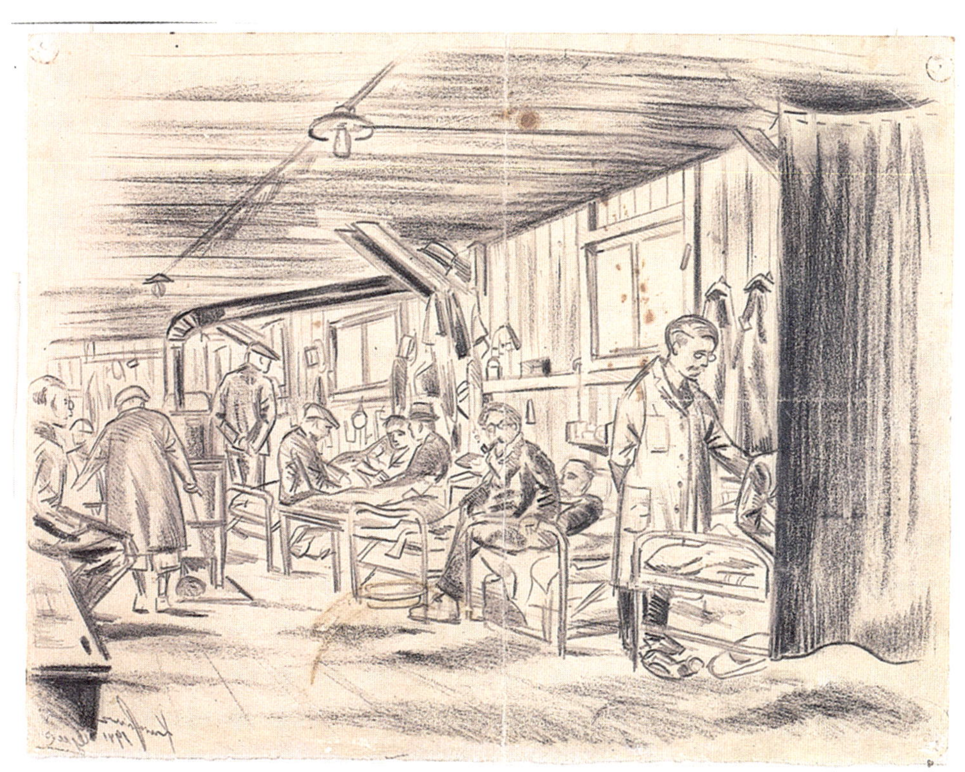

Kurt Prinz
Men's Infirmary, Block B

Dr. Julius Strauss, 1941
Pencil on paper,
30 x 23 cm
Collection of
Yad Vashem Art Museum

the first days at the camp. "However, after a short time I was forbidden to spend the night with my mother. She passed away several days after our arrival, and I saw her death as nothing but an act of kindness. People were dying like flies, most from dysentery. On the day of my mother's burial in early November 1940, the rain and storm were so fierce that it was almost impossible to stand upright. Fourteen people were buried that day, the average number in that period."

Dolly S. described the conditions in the barracks. "Fleas, lice, and rats. The worst, to my mind, were the lice, whose numbers were astronomical. They literally devoured the ill, the feeble, those who had lost the will to live. Sometimes clusters upon clusters of lice – in the millions – clung to clothing, like trousers, hung on the barbed wire fence or in front of the barracks. The entire camp, including, of course, our hut, was infested with rats. Nothing we did deterred these sly creatures, and we took to sleeping with our blankets over our faces."

Amidst this misery, the prisoners demonstrated considerable resourcefulness. The women took up needlework not only to mend their few articles of clothing but also to occupy themselves. Craftsmen who were now idle channeled their creative energy into practical work. They dismantled unoccupied, broken-down huts and used the material to repair their barracks, and there were those who turned tin cans into eating utensils and scrap metal into knives, spoons, strainers, plates, candlesticks, frames, and even mirrors.

Yitzhak K. reports on an initiative taken by his father and some of his friends which led to the opening of a post office in the camp:

"Father requested permission to establish contact between the different living areas of the camp as we did not know how the women and girls were faring. He obtained two passes from headquarters for my friends and me, and we were called *Block Post*. We had permission to move around on the camp's main road and to enter and exit all the blocks, and we would deliver letters and small objects from the men's area to the women's. We utilized this opportunity to purchase food tins and dried fruits for our block from the Spanish prisoners who were allowed to work outside the camp."

The boys found a way to smuggle several loaves of bread into the camp:

"My friends and I discovered a cemetery at the end of the main road, through which one could leave the camp. We related this to our fathers, took money, and dared to leave in order to bring back food for our block. We got to the Gurs village but we didn't speak French. One of the farmers showed us to a barn where we met a woman, a refugee from Belgium, who spoke Yiddish and told us that it was also hard to obtain bread in the village. Nevertheless, her son accompanied us to the local baker who felt sorry for us and sold us a few loaves of bread."

Osias Hofstatter
Prisoners in the camp, 1944

Pen and ink on paper, 30.5 x 24 cm
Collection of Yad Vashem Art Museum
Donated by Dr. Pinhas Rothschild

The bread was handed over to the adults and one of them, well-trusted by his fellow prisoners, cut it into equal pieces. One could learn a lot about people from observing them while the bread was being divided. More than one fight broke out over this, and those intent, quiet looks – checking, studying each crumb – were concentrated on the knife and the size of each piece that was sliced.

All Jews Are Responsible For One Another

Already in September 1940, even before the arrival of the German Jews at the Gurs camp, Rabbi Shmu'el René Kappel foresaw that the upcoming winter would be very difficult. He discussed this at a rabbinical conference and called for a "defeat of hunger, the Gurs prisoners' worst enemy." He appealed to the Jews of France and America to fulfill their obligation to their unfortunate brethren and establish a special emergency fund that would provide better food, medicine for the sick, and milk for the children and the elderly. He added that "all the mutual-aid organizations, both Jewish and non-Jewish, should be informed of the tragedy that is transpiring at the camp."

When the German Jews and the Saint Cyprien prisoners arrived at Gurs, the Red Cross, OSE, ORT, Joint, and the Quakers, as well as the Swiss Jewish communities undertook to help the inmates.

In his book, *A Jew's Struggle in Occupied France,* Rabbi Kappel relates that the camp commander allowed him freedom of movement in all the blocks of the camp, and in his rounds he was shocked by the tragic sights he encountered:

"I became convinced that in order to save the people from complete deterioration, it was necessary to immediately organize welfare services *within* the camp. I proposed that Rabbi Leo Ansbacher and his associates be placed in charge, and before leaving the camp, I conveyed this to the superintendent and his deputy, in order to guarantee that Rabbi Ansbacher's authority be established. I requested that every allowance be made to enable him to carry out his task efficiently and successfully..."

Rabbi Yehudah Leo Ansbacher recounted that in organizing the Gurs camp, he tried to apply the experience he and his friends had gained in Saint Cyprien before their transfer to Gurs:

"We set up the Central Assistance Committee within the camp, primarily in order to provide support for the weak. We designated a barrack in every section of the camp that would serve as a cultural center, a synagogue, and a post office. We delegated tasks to various Jews, and a representative was chosen from each camp section. The Central Committee involved itself in personal, emotional, and material assistance, and established the rule that anyone who received money or food should contribute a portion of it to others. With the help of the barracks' leaders, the money collected in the camp was set aside to support those in need. In the camp were many wealthy people, such as owners of diamond-polishing workshops from Antwerp, or people who received money from Switzerland. We collected a five-percent 'social' tax based on the money that was received from outside the camp. My brother Max was responsible for purchases and was able to obtain quantities of vegetables which saved people's lives."

The committee members and its head, Rabbi Ansbacher, were well-liked throughout the camp. Officially, Rabbi Ansbacher was rabbi of the camp, but he became its primary spiritual and ethical authority as well. Max Ansbacher, the rabbi's brother, was the head of the purchasing unit; Aryeh Zuckerman held many positions in addition to being in charge of the *hevra kadisha* (Jewish burial society); Dr. Pinhas Rothschild, the educator, was responsible for matters of education and social welfare; Helmut Natan, the devoted secretary of the committee, recorded and documented its decisions; and Evan Cohen and Manfred Bauer saw to the distribution of goods efficiently and with sensitivity.

Hanna Schramm describes the committee's visit to their women's block:

"They put the list that we had prepared of our most urgent requests into their pocket – winter clothes for four hundred women, additional food for the sick and the elderly, and wool for knitting. That evening, Aryeh Zuckerman returned with a big bag of biscuits and figs for the children, and every week – sometimes several times a week – the Central Committee sent each block fruit, bread, figs, some oats, and flour."

The Rescue of the Children

The camp authorities allowed the welfare organizations to explore ways to improve conditions for the children, some of whom were ill. The rescue of the children began soon after, the youngest among them being sent to children's homes or to Jewish families in southern France. However, each rescue involved a tragedy. The mother, whose young child was imprisoned with her in the women's block had to make the difficult decision whether to transfer her child to an unfamiliar place, alone, possibly never to see her again. For the children who were saved, the separation from their mothers and the fact that they never said good-bye to their fathers, who were in another block, scarred them for life. These children, first uprooted from their homes, were now torn from their parents and friends and taken to new, strange surroundings where only French was spoken.

Ehud L. was one of the children who were transferred from the camp by OSE (*Oeuvre de Secours aux Enfants,* Children's Aid Society). He was taken to a children's home in Chabannes, and was then hidden by a French family. He describes the separation from his mother:

"And then I became sick. And when I lay on the wet hay, two French-speaking people came with Mother, who was very pale, and stood by me. Mother lifted me into her arms, hugged me with all her remaining strength and whispered in my ear: 'Go with them, Herbert, they will take you to a good place. They will take care of you and afterwards I will come...' Before I had time to react I was already in the man's hands, and he rushed out of the hut and ran with me to the fence. I don't remember how we crossed the fence. I remember traveling in a truck with many other children. I remember arriving at a big house, which served as a children's shelter. I was seven years old and this was the first time in my life that I lived with children."

Uri L. was twelve years old when, in February, 1941, he was separated

Sigismond Kolos-Vari
Three Girls, Gurs Camp

Ink on paper
Yad Vashem Archives

from his parents and taken, with a group, to a children's home. In the letter his father had given him before his departure, Uri understood that his father had placed all his hopes in his son's release. However, in July of 1941, Uri decided to steal back into Gurs to help his parents. With a sack of potatoes on his shoulders, he traveled by bus to Oloron and from there walked the sixteen kilometers to Gurs. He had no difficulty entering the camp, since the boys imprisoned in Gurs knew the location of all the holes in the fence and were aware of the laxity of the guards. He got to the Red Cross hut, shocking the workers there: "Get out of here at once," scolded one of the women who was afraid he would get caught. Uri was insulted and thought no one wanted him. The meeting with his mother, who was sick, was very moving, but she, too, pleaded with him to leave the camp quickly. He elicited a similar reaction when he visited his father. Uri left, never to see his parents again.

The boys who remained in the camp grew up quickly. They witnessed death on a daily basis and saw the bodies taken by wagon for burial. Rafi P., who was fourteen and stayed with his father in the camp, praised his father's conduct in sparing no effort to maintain good personal hygiene and to retain some semblance of human dignity for himself and his son:

"My father behaved as if the driver from the bank would arrive at any moment to collect him. He also forced me to get up each morning. It was unheard of for him to stay in bed, even though we had nothing to do each day. We got up at 6:30 a.m., went outside to wash up in cold water, did exercises, and polished our shoes. I asked: 'Father, why are we polishing our shoes? It doesn't make sense. We are constantly in mud and yet we polish our shoes?'

"Afterwards, we would go for a walk. We would get ersatz coffee and a piece of bread, and go walking. Father was interested in keeping up our strength. I do not recall him sewing a button at home; at home he never did even the smallest thing. Here he placed the shirt under the blanket to somehow 'iron' it. We washed our own clothes, sometimes using a stone to rub them clean. It was unbelievable. I have the most positive memories of my father."

One particular story, as recounted by Rabbi Ansbacher in his testimony, conveys the concern for the fate and innocence of the young girls who remained in the camp, some without any relatives:

"After the Jewish rescue organization, OSE, brought the children out of the camp and into children's homes in Vichy, France, there remained about twenty-five young girls, aged fifteen and above, some without any family. Mrs. A.S., a French Jewish welfare worker who visited the camp, brought to my attention the fact that the French clerks and policemen had their eyes on the girls. We were afraid that these Frenchmen might tempt the girls, who were suffering from terrible hunger, so we asked the camp commander to allocate a place for cultural activities for them. The commander was kind enough to designate part of one of the huts for this purpose, and was quick to notify his superiors about his role in helping to arrange youth activities in the camp. We turned the area into a club and organized the girls into a group called 'Menorah', which met with us several times a week. On the Sabbath and at prayer services we discussed the weekly Torah portion with them, and during the week we conducted Hebrew language classes. There were girls who did not know a single Hebrew letter, and there were those who, if not for Hitler, would never have known that they were Jewish. Speaking emotionally, if I may, there were times when the girls dreamed they would one day establish a kibbutz in the Land of Israel."

After 'Menorah' was fully functional and there was no fear that the core group would disband, Pinhas Rothschild, who was in charge of the group, and Rabbi Ansbacher sought additional activities for the young girls. The rabbi involved them in his work with the weak and the sick. Two of the girls accompanied him in his walks around the camp and helped him identify those in need of assistance, and others were given different responsibilities. This work enhanced the girls' image in the eyes of the prisoners and, especially, in their own eyes. The sense of satisfaction helped them recover from the trauma of being uprooted from their homes and losing their families.

The separation between men and women was especially difficult. It created a great deal of suffering for married couples and family members who were torn

Fritz Schleifer
Cemetery, Gurs Camp, 1941

Watercolor on paper,
27 x 19.5 cm
Collection of
Yad Vashem Art Museum
Donated by
Dr. Pinhas Rothschild

from each other so cruelly. In order to meet, a couple had to submit a formal request, only a small number of which were approved. This led to many personal tragedies. Funerals were the only times men and women were allowed to see each other without prior approval, so many attended funerals of total strangers. This eased somewhat the edict of separation, and it was common to hear people say, as one young woman wrote to her husband: "Otto dear, do me a favor and come to the funeral service at noon."

A Lyrical Story About the Jews Who Were Transported to Gurs

by An Anonymous Woman

Dear ones... over land and over sea,
To you I dedicate these words, so listen if you please:
At one in the morning, at the height of a storm,
I pour my heart out to you.
With my sisters from Baden, Pfaltz, and Saarland,
From twenty years old to eighty,
Your Marta is shackled with ropes
For days and hours on end in a wooden hut.
On Grandmother's eightieth birthday (October 22, 1940)
We were taken with few belongings, for the time we had was short.

Twenty minutes with my two elderly relatives.
Imperative at such a time to remain fully alert.
Now we must hurry to bring warm blankets and shoes,
And also food for three days.
Grandmother was completely confused, I had to do the work,
Only albums of pain and framed pictures she wanted to take.
And for her shrouds, too, she asked the men –
God, help me.
Even today I have no idea how it happened
That I managed to maintain a certain calm,
And with the two of them, among shouts and calls,
I bade farewell to my land.
We traveled by car to the castle,
Where those from the Rhine and the Enz gathered.
At nine in the evening we began to move, The guards forced us to move quickly.
Amidst the confusion I lost all,
Perspiring, yet freezing from the cold.
At one in the morning they searched for me,
Grandmother monopolized the bathroom,
She vomited all the time in front of everyone.
Grandfather, too, did not sit idle,
Slapping himself on the mouth,
Acting wildly, I cannot describe it to you,
Like someone who wants to chase the people from his bed.
He walked around dressed only in a shirt,
Imagine for yourselves, how embarrassed I was.
Luckily, the train traveled rapidly,
To where? – this, no one knew.
We passed by Rastatt, Offenburg, Breisach, the border.
Where everyone – rich and poor – received two thousand francs.
Everything else remained there, not that I cared.
Belfort, Besançon, Montpellier, Avignon, Lyons,
Perpignan, Toulouse, Oloron.

Eventually we arrived,
After seventy hours we reached our destination.

The trip had sapped much of our energy.
But there was compensation,
The beautiful scenery through which we traveled,
Of this everyone agreed.
Mountains and forests, hilltops and seaside,
After all those hours, our hearts sank.
To Gurs, our new home, we arrived
In the rain, not in the sunlight.
Barrack 31 was empty and desolate,
But mattresses and straw sacks came quickly.
Warm soup, after all that suffering
Tasted better than the most sumptuous feast.
There were no tables or plates,
But we enjoyed eating with our hands out of tin cans.

Stroheimer
In the Gurs Camp, 1940

Pencil on paper
Collection of
Yad Vashem Archives

We received bread and soup,
As well as coffee which perked us up,
Even with beans, tastier than malt,
Or the horrible elder plant.
Apples and cheese we got from the kitchen,
Jam, porridge, and oranges.

Elegant lady, doctor, servant – here all are equal,
Here there are no wealthy and no poor.
Can you lend me a few pairs of socks?
I'll exchange them for a pat of butter.
If you give me some tea, to you I'll give some meat.
Someone with cognac is considered a rich person.
Please do not think we are crying here,
God brings out the sun in its full splendor.
Washing and showering are here a great experience,
A person feels garbed in expensive silk clothing.
And Sabbath eve, as well, with the candles and singing,
And joking and teasing, and carrying the water,
This is our current lot in life.
In the afternoon everyone lines up along the barbed wire fence
To see if one's husband is nearby.
You cannot imagine my joy when I saw mine,
After seventeen days plus several hours.
We received a pass between 2:00 and 6:00.
Our conversation I cannot describe.
It is better that I do not.
This week I cleaned the bathrooms
In exchange for a double portion, but not just that.
They allowed me to visit with Hermann, and it was just wonderful.
Everyone envied my pleasure,
But there was only one woman who joined me in the cleaning.
Grandfather is in the Red Cross hut.
He cried during my visit, but not from pain,
On the contrary, his heart was uplifted,
He is as happy as a child.
Until we will reach New York.
Hilda, Helena, Frieda, and Nettl also send their regards,
Being together helps make life more bearable.
One gives coffee, the other porridge,
One warm water, the other tea.
Write back quickly and good night,
I did the very best I could.

Gurs Camp, November 21, 1940

"In Distress I Called on the Lord"

> *"I never saw such devoutness, such religious fervor as I did in those miserable, cold and damp huts, in those makeshift prayer halls."*
>
> Rabbi Shmu'el René Kappel

Religion played a central role in the daily life at Gurs and was encouraged by the camp authorities, who thought that honoring the prisoners' religious requests would serve to dampen their feelings of resentment and frustration. Religious activity began at Gurs in October 1940 with the arrival of the German Jews, among whom were ten rabbinical scholars and intellectuals. These rabbis, with Rabbi Yehudah Ansbacher as their appointed head, assumed the role of spiritual guardians, and proved a major influence on camp life. The camp rabbinate was allotted a hut at the entrance to Gurs, and religious activity expanded. Classes were established for Jewish history, Bible, and Talmud. Regular prayer services, Sabbath eve gatherings, as well as bar mitzvah, wedding, and circumcision celebrations were held in makeshift synagogues.

Rabbi Ansbacher and his staff were given unrestricted passage within the camp. The rabbi prayed with a different block each Sabbath. He would walk over, conduct the services, deliver a sermon on the events of the day and the weekly Torah reading, and end with soothing words of comfort. Many young people participated in the classes held in the *yeshivah* that Rabbi Ansbacher established and called it, respectfully but with a touch of irony, the *"Bnei Brak Yeshivah,"* referring to both the city in Israel and the "barracks" that comprised the camp.

Dr. Pinhas Rothschild, a native German, was running a children's home in Antwerp when he was arrested in May 1940 and sent to the camp. Rothschild was in charge of welfare assistance at Gurs. He recalls that before Passover 5701

(1941), Rabbi Yehudah Ansbacher, his brother Max and Dr. Yosef Weill, who was a well-known doctor in Strasbourg, turned to Gruel, the French operations officer at the camp. They requested that the Jewish prisoners who refrain from eating bread during Passover be given flour for matzot instead. Gruel promised to do so, but stressed that at the last minute his superior might refuse to allow the request to go through, in which case it would be impossible to allocate the flour even for bread-baking. Gruel required a signed commitment from those interested in matzot, stating their willingness to forego their bread portions during the eight-day holiday. Dr. Rothschild was assigned to collect the signatures and was assisted by the 'Menorah' girls. The girls went to each of the barracks, explaining the risk involved and obtaining the necessary signatures. Approximately eight thousand people signed the document and all were granted matzot for the holiday. For that one *Seder* night 5701 (1941), the men and the women were given permission to celebrate together.

In preparation for that Passover holiday, Aryeh Zuckerman prepared from memory a Haggadah for the camp prisoners. This is the Gurs Haggadah.

On the eve of the holiday, the camp rabbinate publicized a list of products permitted and prohibited during Passover.

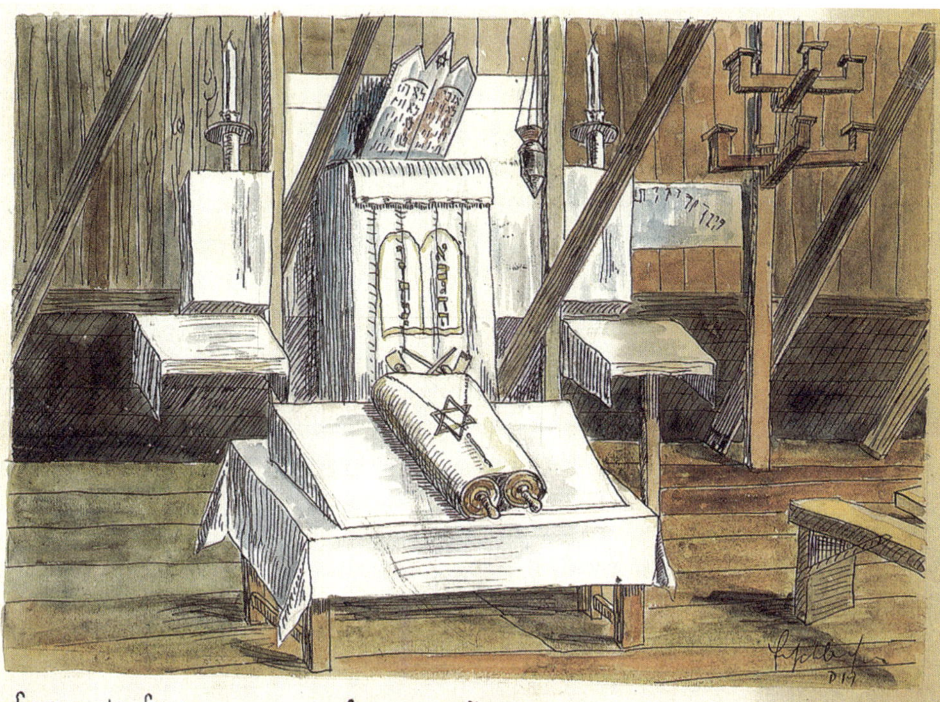

Fritz Schleifer
Gurs Camp,
Rosh Hashana 5702 (1941)

Watercolor, ink on paper
Courtesy of Centre de Documentation Juive Contemporaine (Documentation Center for Contemporary Judaism), Paris

Passover 5701 1941

The following is a list of products which are permitted and prohibited this year:

Prohibited:
Coffee substitute and mixed coffee
Noodles
Semolina
Oat flakes
Chocolate drink "Ovalmaltina," "Blendina" and the like
Bean-corn flour and the like
Tinned spinach
Tomato paste
Bouillon cubes
Beer
Artificial honey
Fish in tomato juice
Cocoa substitute
Tinned low-fat cheese

Permitted:
Saccharin
Tinned vegetables
Legumes
Tinned fish
Canned milk
Jam
Dried fruit
Cheese
Shortening and oil
Chocolate
Pure cocoa
Red wine
Rice is permitted for sick people upon prior approval of the rabbinate.

Additional instructions regarding *hametz*, the *Seder*, kitchen and table utensils will be announced at a later date.

Rabbinical Office Hours: 10:00-11:00 daily, Block G/2, Gurs Camp, 24 March 1941.

Jacob Barosin
Gurs, outside a barrack, sitting idle day after day, cooking a soup as the best remedy for hunger. Enjoying one more day before deportation to the unknown.

Pencil on paper,
17 x 25 cm
Collection of
Yad Vashem Art Museum
Donated by the artist

In 1941, shortly before the High Holy Days, hundreds of pamphlets containing prayers from the *machzorim* (High Holiday prayer books) were distributed. There were *shofars*, Torah scrolls, calendars and *machzorim* in the camp. On Rosh Hashanah the synagogues in the blocks were filled to capacity and thousands of people gathered to hear the shofar. On the eve of Rosh Hashanah, Sunday, September 21, 1941, Rabbi Ansbacher and Rabbi Kappel sent blessings to those imprisoned at Gurs:

Dear Friends,

Rosh Hashanah 5702 comes at a difficult moment for all of us. We are preparing to celebrate the Days of Awe in a manner vastly different from what we expected. Throughout history, the Jewish people knew how to listen to the call of God and to hear His voice even under the most oppressive circumstances. They were able to distinguish, simultaneously, the verdict of the Supreme Judge as well as the trembling cry of the Father for His sons. Only rarely in the Jewish people's long history did the God of our Forefathers call out as clearly as He has done during the course of this past year, now drawing to an end. It is incumbent upon us to give Him an appropriate answer. Let us seriously and honestly ask ourselves if we have fulfilled our obligation to the Lord and to our fellow human beings, whose suffering is ours as well. Let us ask ourselves if we have not neglected many of the spiritual values for which Jews have lived and died throughout generations. Let us ask ourselves if we have not forsaken too much of our true, glorious culture in favor of an alternative which has inflicted such a horrible tragedy upon humanity. And let us not forget that in many places, those who advocate that same "culture" even deprive us of the privilege to take part in it.

Fellow Jews, learn to finally recognize the values of your Judaism. Be assured that if you do so, you will come to respect and treasure them. Facing these severe times and the cruel fate which the hand of the Lord has imposed upon you, be true to your conscience and resolve firmly to return to the Creator. We wish to heed the call of God and to respond to it with all our hearts. We yearn to make an unqualified commitment to fulfill our obligation to God and to each other.

With this deeply rooted faith we stand before the Holy One Blessed Be He on this holy day and bring forth to him our innermost prayers. May He ultimately bless us with a good year, and grant us the strength and health to enable us to return to our homes and see the world at peace.

To you, to us, to our brothers and sisters near and far, we send our most sincere wishes for a *ketiva va-hatima tova* (May you be inscribed and sealed for a good year).

For the fast of Yom Kippur a freight car filled with vegetables was sent to the camp for the pre-fast meal. Due to the lack of space for all the worshippers, the prayers were conducted outdoors. The prayers were recited with great devotion and intense emotion, and thousands fasted.

During the pleasant weather of the *Succot* holiday (Feast of Tabernacles), hundreds filled the public *succah* – a hut whose roof was removed and replaced with *skhakh* (thatched cover). Six additional *succot* were built throughout the camp and artists worked together with the youth to decorate them.

Jacob Barosin
"My bed" Gurs

Pencil on paper,
18 x 25 cm
Collection of
Yad Vashem Art Museum
Donated by the artist

Hannukah 1941 was etched in the prisoners' memories with the lighting of the first candle:

"On the first night of Hannukah we lit the candles in the elderly people's barracks, after the religious ceremony which was held in the cultural hut. There were actually two celebrations that evening because the hut could not accommodate the three hundred participants. There were recitations, songs, opera, and a collection of Jewish folksongs. Afterwards, there was a nice party for the children; we gave them candy and games and there were nothing but happy faces all around."

Osias Hofstatter
Still life, 1944

Pen and ink on paper,
30.5 x 24 cm
Collection of
Yad Vashem Art Museum
Donated by the artist

The following year, on Hannukah 5703 (1942), after the wave of deportations during the summer of 1942 and the arrival of new inmates at the camp, Rabbi Menahem Coriat wrote a poem, "In Honor of the Maccabbees."

The French historian, Claude Laharie, discusses the intense cultural and religious creativity at the Gurs camp, despite the daily hardships:

"Today, many French have difficulty comprehending why the cultural life at Gurs, under the Vichy government, was so vibrant. While admitting that there were some exceptional people among the prisoners, they maintain that the fact that so much energy was invested in activities that were unnecessary for daily existence proves that the prisoners did not suffer as much as they claim.

"This conclusion stems from a deep ignorance of the reality at Gurs. For those in the camp, the normalcy of life ceased to exist and a whole new value system took hold. The nuclear family no longer existed. There were no private dwellings to retreat to. There was no profession to work in and no work to complete. There were no salaries to be earned or a standard of living that had to be maintained.

"What had been essential in the past disappeared, and what was previously viewed as secondary – sewing, artwork, and even religious observance – became the sole purpose of daily existence at Gurs.

"Apathy would have represented a surrender to the pain, the sorrow and the slow loss of human dignity."

The Transports from Gurs to the Death Camps

> *"Those who were sent to the transports exhibited surprising courage. Not all of them knew what end awaited them, but they guessed the truth. There were some decent French guards who shed tears, but they represented a minority."*
>
> Rabbi Yehudah Leo Ansbacher

I now speak my fourth language,
I am in my third country.
I am very worried.
What will become of me I have no idea.
We will soon have to leave, that I know.
My mother is crying today,
She cries a lot and often.
I look sadly at other people
Those who are happy,
I wonder about our next destination,
About the strange cities, the large cities,
There.
I think about the hunger pangs in the evening,
Oh! If only I at least had a friend!
I suffer so much from this loneliness.
Where will we go now?
Will we stay here?
Seven years of wandering, enough!
I have lost my joy.
I am the daughter of an emigree.

Herta Freund

Plans for carrying out the "Final Solution" to the Jewish question were coordinated at the Wannsee Conference of January 20, 1942, which put into effect the deportation of the Jewish population to the extermination centers in the East. On June 11, 1942, while the deportation of the Jews of Western Europe was being discussed, the French authorities committed to transport, as a first step, one hundred thousand Jews from the occupied and unoccupied zones. In the summer of 1942 it was agreed that all the foreign Jews in unoccupied France would be

Jacob Barosin
"The day after the Deportation. The wives come from the women's barracks looking for their husbands. Some find them, some do not..."

Pencil on paper,
25 x 17 cm
Collection of
Yad Vashem Art Museum
Donated by the artist

arrested and sent to the Drancy camp, which would serve as a transit point for those who would then be transported to the east. Adolph Eichmann arrived in Paris in order to implement the program, and a document was drafted whereby France would be made *Judenrein* as soon as possible and the rate of deportation would be significantly stepped up. The Vichy government undertook to hand over thirty thousand foreign Jews to the Germans, mostly those from Germany, Austria, and Poland. Preparations were begun in late July 1942, preceded by anti-Jewish laws initiated by the Vichy regime.

Detailed plans for the deportation were mapped out, as evidenced by what *SS-Hauptsturmfuehrer* Theodor Dannecker, in charge of Jewish affairs in France, wrote:

"The trains will consist of a locomotive, three passenger cars for the policemen, and twenty freight cars.... The French government will cover the expenses of the transport, an overall payment of seven hundred marks for each Jew, as well as food and clothing costs for a fourteen-day period beginning with the date of departure. It would be best to gather the Jews before the deportation. Every convoy will consist of one thousand Jews, one of whom will be appointed in each car to maintain order throughout the journey and clean it afterwards. A pail should be provided in each car for hygienic needs."

Six transports departed from Gurs for the Drancy camp. Beginning August 1942 four convoys of deportees left Gurs, and in February-March 1943 another two were sent. Just before each deportation the camp was surrounded by French police and the designated prisoners were isolated in a separate block, with different barracks for families and for singles. At this stage, too, the welfare associations acted to ease the increased burden. The Committee to Assist the Deportees supplied food for the camp, and the rabbinate gave a sum of money to each family head. A not-insignificant number of prisoners chose to join their spouses who had been assigned to a transport, thus providing a deferment, albeit a temporary one, for others. Panic, hysteria, outbursts, and suicide attempts were common among the deportees. Rabbi Ansbacher reported:

"There was on unfortunate Jew who was unsuccessful at everything he tried. He was a real *shlemazel,* a hopeless case.... One day, during the deportations, a group of people were sitting in a circle and one of them was crying bitterly, pleading for a two day reprieve. He was willing to go on the next transport, to wherever they wanted, if only they would let him stay. His wife and son, whom he had not seen for three years, had notified him that they were scheduled to arrive the next day. While there were those who volunteered to go to their death together with their families, he was pleading to be allowed to see his wife and then he would prepared to go.... With just a half-hour left before his departure, he looked around the circle hoping that someone would agree to go in his place, but no one offered.

Then this *schlemazel* said: "I will go in your place."

The activities of the 'Menorah' girls, which had begun in the winter of 1941, ceased in the summer of 1942 when the transports left Gurs for the extermination camps. Of the whole group, only three girls survived.

Rabbi Ansbacher told of Marian, the oldest of the Menorah girls, who had initially hesitated to participate in their activities, but eventually became the assistant to The Committee to Assist the Deportees and to the rabbinate, and joined in the discussion of the weekly Torah portion:

"Marian and her mother appeared on the first list of evacuees. On the day of evacuation, all were given a short time to say goodbye. Throughout that morning we worked to help them and I went around trying to lend support and encouragement. At one o'clock in the afternoon, in their last moments at the camp, I sat, totally desolate, in the rabbinate's hut.

"The door opened and Marian stood in the entrance. I have no idea how she obtained the lipstick and colorful sweater that she wore. She looked, as they say in Yiddish, *yomtovdik (*holiday-ish). I asked, 'Marian, do you think this is appropriate?' And she answered in a choked voice: 'Yes, you know, right now I recall all the troubles we had, all the suffering we went through, but of one thing I am certain: This is the first place that I am sorry to leave.'

"And she left.

- לכבוד המכבים הקדושים -

הלנו כבוד למכבים הגבורים !
הזקן מתתיהו עם הבנים .
שנלחמו כאריות נגד היונים .
אויבים עזים וקשים כעמלקים .
אשר חשבו לאבד היהודים .
ולהכרית זרעם מבין העמים .
טמאו בפסילים בית הקדשים .
חרפו וגדפו דת האלהים .
לקרב יצאו חשמונאים הנאים .
לבם ועינם לשמים מביטים .
דגל יהודה מרימים בהלולים .
מכבי מכבי שם חקוקים .
מי כמוך באלים ה' משוררים .
נצחו הכהנים ליונים הרשעים .
גבורת המכבים חזקים כפטישים .
נפל פחדם על היונים .
חזרו הכהנים ממלחמתם עליזים .
דגלים עברו בחוצות ירושלים .

נצחון ! נצחון העם צועקים .
קומו ! לעזרת ה' בגבורים !
מרננים כהנים לוים וישראלים .
נכנסים למקדש בתשבחות ושירים .
טהרוהו וחנכוהו לריח ניחחים .
הדליקו הנרות בשמנים טהורים .
כבדו את ה' באורים .
ועלו האורות עד לשחקים .
התפללו לה' צבאות על הנסים .
והמשכילים יזהירו כזוהר הרקיעים .
במצות חנוכה סוד קדושים .
החשמונאים נתנו לנו הסמנים .
מדליקין חנוכה שמונה ימים .
תקות משיח שם רמוזים .
נתן כבוד לכהנים הצדיקים .
נשמתם כנצוצים נלהבים מבהיקים .
משפיעים עלינו תמיד ומאירים .
יבורך זכרם לנצח נצחים :

"They did not allow us to leave the block. I stood with those left behind, watching the deportees on the road that divided the camp. We forced our way past the chain of guards. Marian walked, looking at us the whole time, the smile never leaving her face."

Rabbi Kappel was present during the deportation from the camp, and writes in his memoirs:

הו ! בני המכבים אחים ורעים .
עורו ! למדו עברית שפת ההורים .
מורשה לנו מבריאת העולמים .
בידיעת שפתנו נגאלנו ממצרים .
ובזכותה חקוים להיות נגאלים .
נשובה לציון ! כימי קדומים .
שובו ! שובו ! ממרחקים לארץ העברים .
נשאף אויר רוחני ממעונים .
נרימה הדגלים ! בזמירות וגילים .
ואז נשיר שירים חדשים .
ה' מי כמוך באלים :

פואימה שעשה הרב פרופיסור
מנחם קוריאט
Rabbin Prof. M. CORIAT
- לכבוד המכבים הקדושים -
בחגיגת חנוכה של מחנה הסגר גורס
שנה תש"ב לפ"ק

"The transfer from Gurs to the train station at Oloron Saint Marie began at midnight and concluded before daybreak. The bus shuttled back and forth through the night while a light rain fell incessantly over the whole region. It is impossible to forget the cry of despair, like the howl of a wounded animal, that came from a father when his seventeen-year old daughter passed his block. The father remained at the camp, while the daughter, who was listed among the deportees, walked to the bus at the camp entrance. The beautiful, charming and blond-haired daughter responded to this call of terror with one word: 'Papa,' which was lost in the shroud-like fog blanketing that abominable place. This horrific scene plagues me to this day."

Among the documents from Gurs collected by Dr. Pinhas Rothschild in the first years after the Holocaust was a paper signed by Dr. Yitzhak Eugen Neter with the following account which he wrote for posterity:

"In early 1943, fifty to sixty internees were assembled in each barrack. Two officers read out names from a list. The 1,080 people whose names were announced moved to one side and were taken afterwards to a round-up hut for the transfer eastward.

"Then the following incident occurred in one of the women's barracks: During the reading of the names, the officers called out the name 'Anna Simone,' but a different woman showed up at the assembly point. Mrs. Simone remained behind and was, therefore, saved from deportation. The woman who took her place had heard that her husband was designated for transport, and she chose to share his fate. I later met the two of them in the hut intended for those to be transported to the east.

"The welfare organizations began immediate rescue attempts, hoping to utilize criteria that would exempt as many as possible from deportation. On many occasions, Rabbi Shmu'el René Kappel managed to obtain forged documents which would be used by prisoners who escaped. After the first deportation there were increased attempts to escape, and those who succeeded were assisted outside the camp by resistance groups and found hiding places in France. Others crossed the Pyrenees mountain range into Spain.

Rabbi Ansbacher was also involved in the escape attempts and was consequently imprisoned, his appointment as rabbi revoked. His name was included in the list of deportees, and it was therefore decided to smuggle him out. He succeeded in crossing the Pyrenees and found refuge in Spain. Dr. Pinhas Rothschild and Max Ansbacher left the camp with the help of visas, to Switzerland. Aryeh Zuckerman escaped, hidden in a coffin, assisted by one of his French acquaintances. Adele K. and the boys Yitzhak, Binyamin and Rafi had been moved to other camps before the deportations began. Lisa P. escaped to Spain in 1940 and was active in smuggling other prisoners out of the camp.

Dr. Yitzhak Neter was among the few who were permitted to remain in the Gurs camp:

"Due to the high incidence of deaths, transfers to other camps, and the deportations, the number of inmates at Gurs was reduced to less than one thousand. Only a few remained of the Baden and Pfaltz deportees. The barracks stood empty and the camp road was deserted. Those left behind took over the vacated barracks and recalled with horror their first days here at Gurs. The nightmare of the monotonous hell receded; only the hunger and the barbed wire remained."

Dr. Neter was smuggled out of the camp in 1943 and found sanctuary in an old-age home in France.

Epilogue

At the end of the war, Dr. Pinhas Rothschild returned to his family in Brussels and managed an orphanage. One day, a man from the Jewish Brigade, a tall and handsome young soldier with blond hair, chanced into the place. He had come to evaluate the needs of the institution and suggested that perhaps the soldiers from the land of Israel might be able to assist in locating children who had been taken to monasteries and foster homes.

"What is your name?" asked Dr. Rothschild, overcome at the sight of him.

"Sha'ul Neter," answered the soldier.

"I knew a man named Dr. Eugen Neter," said Rothschild.

"Is he alive?" inquired Sha'ul.

This was indeed the son of Dr. Yitzhak Eugen Neter, who had moved to Eretz Israel before the war, joined the British army and later the Jewish Brigade with which he had come to Europe. Sha'ul knew nothing of his father's fate and only succeeded in finding him after first meeting his mother in Mannheim. His parents moved to Eretz Israel, joining him in Kibbutz Degania. Later, Dr. Rothschild also moved to Eretz Israel. Here he heard that Sha'ul Neter had a baby boy, and he sent him a congratulatory note. He received, in response, a letter from Dr. Yitzhak Neter containing the heartbreaking news that his only son had been killed in the battle for Degania three months after the birth of his grandson.

Sha'ul fell on 9 Iyar 5708 (May 18, 1948), while posted at the forward position opposite the Syrian forces which had reached the kibbutz fence.

Dr. Yitzhak Eugen Neter, known in Degania as "Grandpa Neter," lived a long life and passed away on 24 Tishrei 5727 (October 8, 1966), just before his 90th birthday.

Benny (Ben Zion), Sha'ul's son, was drafted into the IDF and served in the Engineering Corps. Benny Neter fell at the age of twenty in the Karame action on 21 Adar 5728 (March 21, 1968).

Three graves now stand side by side in the cemetery at Degania, the three generations of Neters.

19
Berkefeld

Researching the Gurs Haggadah

Tirza Oren

The religious enthusiasm expressed by the prisoners in the camp was the most sincere imaginable. The depth and vigor of religious belief often surprised and moved a new arrival. The effect of hearing poignant, improvised prayers, both personal and congregational, coming from the corner of a hut or in the darkness of the locked cattle truck in which we were brought back from a distant work site – tired, hungry and frozen in our ragged clothing – left the listener filled with awe.

Viktor Frankl, *Man's Search for Meaning*, p.54

Over the years, testimony was collected at Yad Vashem regarding the religious life of the Jews and their attempts to preserve Jewish tradition and holidays during 1933-1945. This documentation included objects, written evidence, and oral testimonies. One example of this is the Passover Haggadah that was written at the Gurs detention camp in France before Passover 5701 (1941). While doing research for the new Historical Museum at Yad Vashem, I discovered the Gurs Haggadah, written on both sides of five pages, lying in a box in the archives. The Haggadah consists of hand-written pages in block letters, and an additional page that includes several of the songs and hymns from the Haggadah typed in Latin letters. A line in French appears at the end of this page, stating: "Edited by the rabbinate, Rabbi Leo Ansbacher, Gurs (France), *Nissan* 5701 (1941)."

At first glance it looked as if the Haggadah was incomplete, and if that was the case, where were the missing sections? Had they gotten lost?

A check of the archives list showed that the Haggadah had been submitted to Yad Vashem in the 1950s. Investigations, even those related to the Historical Museum of Yad Vashem, always include an element of "detective work"; the nature of the work requires that it be conducted with great care and sensitivity. And so it was with the Gurs Haggadah. Various searches led me to Mr. Mordecai Ansbacher, the museum's first director, who referred me to Rabbi Yehudah Leo Ansbacher. At the time of the Haggadah's production, Rabbi Ansbacher was imprisoned at Gurs and served as its rabbi. After immigrating to Israel, Rabbi Ansbacher was the rabbi of the "*Ihud Shivat Zion*" congregation in Tel Aviv for many years, until his death in the summer of 5758 (1998). At the funeral it was noted

that Rabbi Ansbacher was not accustomed to formalities and was able to establish a warm relationship with each member of his congregation. This reminded me of the warmth with which he had received me two years earlier. At that meeting he spoke extensively about life in Frankfurt before the Nazis' rise to power, his emigration from Germany to Belgium in 1933, his arrest and deportation to France in May 1940, his immigration to Israel via Spain, and especially about his detention in Gurs. The archives at Yad Vashem contain some of Rabbi Ansbacher's oral and written testimonies.

I brought photocopies of the Haggadah to my meeting with Rabbi Ansbacher. After studying them he said that nothing was missing or lost, and that the Haggadah which was written in Gurs was incomplete. It was handwritten by Aryeh Ludwig Zuckerman over many months and under harsh conditions. When the Passover holiday was approaching and the writing not yet finished, it was decided to type the songs and hymns using a typewriter with Latin letters since one with Hebrew letters was unavailable. Not all of the songs had been typed by the time Passover arrived, so the Haggadah was left incomplete. Ultimately, the part printed in Latin letters proved helpful for those who were unable to read Hebrew. According to Rabbi Ansbacher, it seems that Aryeh Zuckerman did not have a Haggadah from which to copy, so he had to write everything from memory. Mr. Zuckerman passed away in Belgium in 1958, and Rabbi Ansbacher suggested that I approach his son, Rabbi A. Yehoshu'a Zuckerman.

Rabbi Ansbacher elaborated about that Passover in Gurs. For the last day of Passover they received permission to prepare an area outside the camp that was large enough to conduct a prayer service for all of the inmates. That was one of the few occasions when they were permitted to do this. The rabbi himself conducted the service in the open area and also delivered a sermon during the *Yizkor* prayer.[1] Rabbi Ansbacher recalled that after the holiday one of the artists who were imprisoned at Gurs painted this event. The painting was preserved and submitted to Yad Vashem by Dr. Pinhas Sigfried Rothschild, who also handed over much archival material about Gurs.

The painting is 27 x 24 cm, done in watercolor on paper, and in it a man (Rabbi Ansbacher) is standing on a platform, surrounded by a large crowd of people, delivering a sermon. On the right side of the painting is the artist's signature, Fritz Schleifer, and underneath the painting, on the left side, appears the Hebrew word *Mazkir.*[2] Written in the center, in German, is: "Dedicated to the esteemed rabbi of the camp, Mr. Leo Ansbacher." On the left side is written: "CAMP de GURS, PESSACH (*Passover*), 1941, ILOT D."

Religious life in the Gurs camp, as well as Rabbi Ansbacher's activities, are discussed by Rabbi Shmu'el René Kappel in his book, *A Jew's Struggle in Occupied France*. Rabbi Kappel was drafted as a chaplain in the French army as soon as the Second World War broke out. After his release he was appointed welfare rabbi of the detention camps in southwest France. The late Rabbi Kappel was a central figure in preserving the memories of life in the Gurs camp. He wrote:

"In early January 1941, I paid another visit to Gurs. I suggested to Leo Ansbacher and his assistants that they establish a committee to centralize the religious, social, and cultural activities of the camp. Thus was formed the *Comite Central d'Assistance – C.C.A.*, which deserves high praise for the tireless work of its members, among them Leo Ansbacher, his brother Max, who was a dynamic and efficient organizer, Aryeh Zuckerman... Dr. Sigfried Rothschild....

"On Passover eve, a large congregation would gather in the barracks where the age-old Passover ceremony would take place. It was Rabbi Leo Ansbacher who was deemed worthy of organizing religious life in the camp. On Sabbaths and holidays Ansbacher himself led the prayers and would often deliver encouraging and comforting sermons."

The printing of the Haggadah for the prisoners was a major accomplishment. From its appearance and by all accounts, it seems that Aryeh Zuckerman wrote the Haggadah on stencils.[3] Rabbi Ansbacher referred me to the copy of the Gurs Haggadah found in the National Library at the Hebrew University, and to the book by Avraham Ya'ari, *Bibliography of Passover Haggadot From the Beginning of Printing Until Today*, which was published in 5721 (1961). In the chapter, "Haggadah in the Holocaust and After," Ya'ari writes:

"In 1941, in the south of France, which was ruled by the Vichy government, two Haggadahs were printed under extremely harsh conditions. One was written for the many Jewish refugees, concentrated in Nice, who had fled German-occupied northern France. The other was written for the inmates of the concentration camp in Gurs.... The Gurs Haggadah was edited by Rabbi Leo Ansbacher, himself a prisoner (and who now lives in the state of Israel). The hymns at the end of the Haggadah... were transliterated and typed in Latin letters, certainly to allow those who could not read Hebrew to participate in the singing...."

Ya'ari goes on to describe the Gurs Haggadah itself:

"Handwritten in block letters with appropriate vowels and copied on a duplicating machine. The last page (which includes the hymns *Ki Lo Na'eh, El Bneh, Ehad Mi Yode'ah, and Had Gadya*) was typewritten in Latin letters...."

In 5757 (1997) the book *A Treasury of Haggadot – Bibliography of Passover Haggadot from the Beginning of Printing Until 5720 (1960)*, edited by Yitzhak Yodlov, was published. Yodlov followed Ya'ari's lead and included a description of the Gurs Haggadah:

"Printed without a title page. Duplicated from a handwritten manuscript. The last page includes the hymns *Ki Lo Na'eh, Adir Hu, Ehad Mi Yode'ah,* and *Had Gadya* typewritten in Latin letters. The Haggadah was written especially for the refugees at that place."

Rabbi Kappel also described the Passover holiday in Gurs and the duplication of the Haggadah:

"Before the Passover holiday... I brought an abbreviated version of the Haggadah, one that had been very well-prepared by Aryeh Zuckerman, to Toulouse for duplication. Thus, all the participants in the *Seder* could express their faith in the Rock of Israel while singing the traditional tunes of *Ehad Mi Yode'ah* or *Had Gadya.* As a gesture of appreciation, *Comite Central d'Assistance* representatives presented me with a copy of the Haggadah, which I keep in my library in Jerusalem. On the last page of that Haggadah is a watercolor painting of Rabbi Ansbacher standing on the platform while delivering a sermon during the *Yizkor* prayer. Surrounding him are throngs of people, deep in thought. The snow-covered Pyrenees Mountains are painted on the horizon. The dedication on the first page reads: May God redeem us, to a friend of us all, Gurs Camp, Passover 1941."

When looking at the Haggadah and at the pictures that Fritz Schleifer painted, it is difficult to imagine the circumstances under which they were created. Yoseph Haim Yerushalmi includes facsimile copies of two pages from the Gurs Haggadah in his book *Haggadah and History*.

Yerushalmi wrote: "A one-line colophon[4] with scant details appears at the bottom of the last page... there is no reference to the tragic circumstances under which the Haggadah was written."

When comparing the Haggadah in Yad Vashem's archives with other copies which we have seen, it is clear that all the copies are identical (including the special copies described below). The Haggadah consists of five pages written in Hebrew, and another page with several *Seder* songs printed in Latin letters. The pages are 21 x 27 centimeters.

The Haggadah is not complete and the same mistake appears in all the copies: The second page opens with "With a mighty hand," whose real place in the Haggadah is after "I, and no messenger; I, Hashem (God), it is I and no other," i.e., on the sixth page. Indeed, the number six is written in pencil on this page in several of the copies.

Mr. Meir Hovav wrote a newspaper article in *HaTzofeh* about the Gurs Haggadah, in which he refers to this mistake: "Apparently, the Haggadah was written on stencils which were taken from the camp for duplication by outsiders. So it transpired that the second page opens with the words 'With a mighty hand,' although it belongs on the sixth page. Aside from that flaw, all the other pages are printed in the correct order." This explanation for the error is undoubtedly correct.

In order to clarify the circumstances surrounding the writing of the Gurs Haggadah, we met with Dr. Pinhas Rothschild, Max Ansbacher and his son Shimon, and with Rabbi A. Yehoshu'a Zuckerman – the son of the late Aryeh Zuckerman, the man who wrote the Haggadah.

Like Rabbi Ansbacher, Dr. Pinhas Rothschild emigrated from Germany to Belgium, where he was arrested and deported to France in May 1940. He was active in the *Comite Central d'Assistance* at Gurs, and was in charge of welfare assistance to the prisoners. When asked if they sang the songs of the Haggadah, he answered, "Yes. We did not cry all the time." He added that it is possible that the Haggadah was written economically as there was not enough paper. Regarding the prayer service depicted in Fritz Schleifer's painting, he stressed that it was a special and extraordinary event, open to everyone who wanted to join. Concerning the painting, he said that the artist had, of course, added color that was not there in reality: "Gurs was not a *rose garden*."

Dr. Rothschild has a copy of the Gurs Haggadah, the last page of which has dedications to him written by Rabbi Ansbacher and Aryeh Zuckerman, the man who wrote the Haggadah. Meir Hovav, who, as stated above, wrote an article about this Haggadah in *HaTzofeh*, saw Dr. Rothschild's copy.

Max Ansbacher, Rabbi Ansbacher's brother, was also deported from Belgium to France. His job at Gurs was an organizational one; he was the liaison among the various welfare associations. He conveyed to us, via his son Mr. Shimon Ansbacher, that as far as he could recall, the Haggadah was written on stencils and duplicated outside of the camp.

Rabbi A. Yehoshu'a Zuckerman, the son of the author of the Gurs Haggadah,

Edité du Rabbinat du Rabbin LEO ANSBACHER, GURS (France) NISSAN 5701.

Der Lichtblick in dieser Zeit, waren die Freunde, die wir getroffen.

A notre Ami Julien Samuel - au chasseur infatigable des nourritures supplémentaires

פותח את ידך ומשביע

Souvenir de Pesach 5701

related that his father, Aryeh Zuckerman, was born in Germany and emigrated to Belgium in 1924; in May 1940 he was arrested and deported to France. At Gurs he concerned himself with caring for the sick, education, organizing religious life and Torah learning, and with the *Chevra Kadisha* (Jewish burial society). Rabbi Zuckerman has the copy of the Haggadah given to him by his father. He remembers his father telling him that he had written the Haggadah from memory, and had apparently used a sharpened stone as a stylus to impress the stencils.

Special Copies of the Gurs Haggadah

The Julien Samuel Copy

The Yad Vashem Museum's collection includes a special copy of the Gurs Haggadah, received by Julien Samuel in appreciation for his assistance to the prisoners there. Julien Samuel was a French Jew from Alsace who was active in OSE (*Oeuvre de Secours Aux Enfants*; Children's Aid Society). According to all accounts the food at Gurs was very meager and Julien Samuel helped the prisoners obtain additional food.

On the last page of this copy of the Haggadah is a dedication signed by Rabbi Ansbacher, Aryeh Zuckerman, Dr. Rothschild, and Max Ansbacher. In Hebrew is written: "You open Your Hand and feed [every creature]" (Psalms 145:16). In German, the sentence: "During this period the friends we acquired were a ray of light for us." In French: "To our friend, Julien Samuel, the inexhaustible provider of additional food." On the first page is a watercolor by Fritz Schleifer, depicting Rabbi Ansbacher speaking before a large crowd, similar to the picture described earlier, with minor differences. The picture is 19 x 13 centimeters. Written underneath it is: "Gurs Camp, Sermon by Our Teacher, Rabbi Y. Ansbacher, Passover 5701, *Mazkir*."

Julien Samuel's family submitted this copy of the Haggadah to the Yad Vashem

Museum in 1983. It was displayed, along with the painting by Fritz Schleifer, at the Historical Museum of Yad Vashem during Passover 5758 (1998).

The Rabbi Samuel Kappel Copy

Rabbi Kappel passed away in Jerusalem in 5754 (1994). His copy of the Haggadah resides with his daughter, Mrs. Yehudit Blum. This copy has a dedication by Rabbi Ansbacher and a similar Fritz Schleifer painting in which Rabbi Ansbacher is seen lecturing. The painting is 19 x 14 centimeters.

The Archive Copy in England

At Rabbi Ansbacher's memorial service, mention was made of another copy of the Haggadah which was discovered purely by chance in the *genizah* of a synagogue in England. The person who found this copy noticed the name Ansbacher and had it brought to the family.

Underneath the picture that Fritz Schleifer painted in Gurs on Passover 5701 is written: "Dedicated to the esteemed rabbi of the camp, Mr. Leo Ansbacher." There is much testimony about Rabbi Ansbacher's special talents as a rabbi and as a social worker in the difficult conditions of the Gurs camp. His students and congregants in Israel relate that the Rabbi mentioned the Holocaust in every one of his sermons, but did not speak of himself very often. Thus it happened that only at his memorial service did many of them first hear about the Gurs Haggadah, a facsimile copy of which is reproduced in this book.

---

[1] *Yizkor* prayer – A prayer commemorating the souls of relatives who have passed away, recited by *Ashkenazi* Jews after the Torah reading on Yom Kippur, Simhat Torah, the last day of Passover, and Shavu'ot.

[2] Some German communities refer to *Yizkor* as *Mazkir*.

[3] A special kind of paper treated with wax or similar material, made in such a way that whatever is written on it with a stylus or typewriter, can be duplicated.

[4] A concluding note by the person who copies a manuscript. It was customary to add information such as the name of the copier, the place, the date, etc., at the end of a book or manuscript.

עברה אחת, וזעם שתים, וצרה שלש, משלחת מלאכי רעים ארבע. אמור מעתה במצרים לקו ארבעים מכות ועל הים לקו מאתים מכות:

רבי עקיבא אומר מנין שכל מכה ומכה שהביא הקדוש ברוך הוא על המצריים במצרים היתה של חמש מכות, שנאמר ישלח בם חרון אפו עברה וזעם וצרה משלחת מלאכי רעים: חרון אפו אחת. עברה שתים. וזעם שלש. וצרה ארבע. משלחת מלאכי רעים חמש. אמור מעתה במצרים לקו חמשים מכות. ועל הים לקו חמשים ומאתים מכות:

כמה מעלות טובות למקום עלינו:

אלו הוציאנו ממצרים. ולא עשה בהם שפטים. דיינו:
אלו עשה בהם שפטים. ולא עשה באלהיהם. דיינו:
אלו עשה באלהיהם. ולא הרג את בכוריהם. דיינו:
אלו הרג את בכוריהם. ולא נתן לנו את ממונם. דיינו:
אלו נתן לנו את ממונם. ולא קרע לנו את הים. דיינו:
אלו קרע לנו את הים. ולא העבירנו בתוכו בחרבה. דיינו:
אלו העבירנו בתוכו בחרבה. ולא שקע צרינו בתוכו. דיינו:
אלו שקע צרינו בתוכו. ולא ספק צרכנו במדבר ארבעים שנה
אלו ספק צרכנו במדבר ארבעים שנה. ולא האכילנו את המן. דיינו:
אלו האכילנו את המן. ולא נתן לנו את השבת. דיינו:
אלו נתן לנו את השבת. ולא קרבנו לפני הר סיני. דיינו:
אלו קרבנו לפני הר סיני. ולא נתן לנו את התורה. דיינו:
אלו נתן לנו את התורה. ולא הכניסנו לארץ ישראל. דיינו:
אלו הכניסנו לארץ ישראל. ולא בנה לנו את בית הבחירה. דיינו:

על אחת כמה וכמה טובה כפולה ומכפלת למקום עלינו: שהוציאנו ממצרים ועשה בהם שפטים ועשה באלהיהם והרג את בכוריהם ונתן לנו את ממונם וקרע לנו את הים והעבירנו בתוכו בחרבה ושקע צרינו בתוכו וספק צרכנו במדבר ארבעים שנה והאכילנו את המן ונתן לנו את השבת

וקרבנו לפני הר סיני ונתן לנו את התורה והכניסנו לארץ ישראל. ובנה לנו את בית הבחירה לכפר על כל עונותינו:

רבן גמליאל היה אומר כל שלא אמר שלשה דברים אלו בפסח. לא יצא ידי חובתו ואלו הן פסח, מצה, מרור:

פסח שהיו אבותינו אוכלים בזמן שבית המקדש קים על שום מה על שום שפסח הקדוש ברוך הוא על בתי אבותינו במצרים שנאמר ואמרתם זבח פסח הוא ליי אשר פסח על בתי בני ישראל במצרים בנגפו את מצרים ואת בתינו הציל ויקד העם וישתחוו:

מצה זו שאנו אוכלים על שום מה. על שום שלא הספיק בצקם של אבותינו להחמיץ עד שנגלה עליהם מלך מלכי המלכים הקדוש ברוך הוא וגאלם. שנאמר ויאפו את הבצק אשר הוציאו ממצרים עגת מצות כי לא חמץ כי גרשו ממצרים ולא יכלו להתמהמה וגם צדה לא עשו להם:

מרור זה שאנו אוכלים על שום מה. על שום שמררו המצרים את חיי אבותינו במצרים. שנאמר וימררו את חייהם בעבודה קשה בחמר ובלבנים ובכל עבדה בשדה את כל עבדתם אשר עבדו בהם בפרך:

בכל דור ודור חיב אדם לראות את עצמו כאלו הוא יצא ממצרים שנאמר והגדת לבנך ביום ההוא לאמר בעבור זה עשה יי לי בצאתי ממצרים: לא את אבותינו בלבד גאל הקדוש ברוך הוא אלא אף אותנו גאל עמהם שנאמר ואותנו הוציא משם למען הביא אתנו לתת לנו את הארץ אשר נשבע לאבתינו:

לפיכך אנחנו חיבים להודות להלל לשבח לפאר לרומם להדר לברך לעלה ולקלס למי שעשה לאבותינו ולנו את כל הנסים האלו. הוציאנו מעבדות לחרות. מיגון לשמחה ומאבל ליום טוב. ומאפלה לאור גדול. ומשעבוד לגאלה. ונאמר לפניו שירה חדשה הללויה:

קאמפ דע גורס

מזכיר

דרשה של
מוה"ר י' אנסבאכער
פסח תשא'

ב"ה

הגדה על פסח

קדש
ורחץ
כרפס
יחץ
מגיד
רחצה
מוציא
מצה

מרור כורך שלחן עורך צפון ברך הלל נרצה

(יום הששי. ויכלו השמים והארץ וכל צבאם: ויכל אלהים ביום השביעי מלאכתו אשר עשה. וישבת ביום השביעי מכל מלאכתו אשר עשה: ויברך אלהים את יום השביעי ויקדש אתו כי בו שבת מכל מלאכתו אשר ברא אלהים לעשות.:) ב"א י"י א"מ"ה" בורא פרי הגפן:
ב"א י"י א"מ"ה" אשר בחר בנו מכל עם ורוממנו מכל לשון וקדשנו במצותיו. ותתן לנו י"י אלהינו באהבה (שבתות למנוחה ו) מועדים לשמחה חגים וזמנים לששון את יום (השבת הזה ואת יום) חג המצות הזה. זמן חרותינו (באהבה) מקרא קדש זכר ליציאת מצרים. כי בנו בחרת ואותנו קדשת מכל העמים (ושבת) ומועדי קדשך (באהבה וברצון) בשמחה ובששון הנחלתנו. ברוך אתה י"י מקדש (השבת ו) ישראל והזמנים: (ב"א י"י א"מ"ה" בורא מאורי האש
ב"א י"י א"מ"ה" המבדיל בין קדש לחול בין אור לחשך בין ישראל לעמים בין יום השביעי לששת ימי המעשה. בין קדשת שבת לקדשת יום טוב הבדלת ואת יום השביעי מששת ימי המעשה קדשת. הבדלת וקדשת את עמך ישראל בקדשתך. ב"א י"י המבדיל בין קדש לקדש:
ב"א י"י א"מ"ה" שהחינו וקימנו והגיענו לזמן הזה:
ב"א י"י א"מ"ה" בורא פרי האדמה:

הא לחמא עניא די אכלו אבהתנא בארעא דמצרים. כל דכפין ייתי ויכול. כל דצריך ייתי ויפסח. השתא הכא לשנה הבאה בארעא דישראל. השתא עבדי לשנה הבאה בני חורין:

בְּיָד חֲזָקָה זו הַדֶּבֶר כְּמָה שֶׁנֶּאֱמַר הִנֵּה יַד יְיָ הוֹיָה בְּמִקְנְךָ אֲשֶׁר בַּשָּׂדֶה בַּסּוּסִים בַּחֲמֹרִים בַּגְּמַלִּים בַּבָּקָר וּבַצֹּאן דֶּבֶר כָּבֵד מְאֹד: וּבִזְרֹעַ נְטוּיָה זו הַחֶרֶב. כְּמָה שֶׁנֶּאֱמַר וְחַרְבּוֹ שְׁלוּפָה בְּיָדוֹ נְטוּיָה עַל יְרוּשָׁלָיִם: וּבְמֹרָא גָּדֹל זו גִּלּוּי שְׁכִינָה כְּמָה שֶׁנֶּאֱמַר אוֹ הֲנִסָּה אֱלֹהִים לָבוֹא לָקַחַת לוֹ גוֹי מִקֶּרֶב גּוֹי בְּמַסֹּת בְּאֹתֹת וּבְמוֹפְתִים וּבְמִלְחָמָה וּבְיָד חֲזָקָה וּבִזְרוֹעַ נְטוּיָה וּבְמוֹרָאִים גְּדֹלִים כְּכֹל אֲשֶׁר עָשָׂה לָכֶם יְיָ אֱלֹהֵיכֶם בְּמִצְרַיִם לְעֵינֶיךָ: וּבְאֹתוֹת זה הַמַּטֶּה כְּמָה שֶׁנֶּאֱמַר וְאֶת הַמַּטֶּה הַזֶּה תִּקַּח בְּיָדֶךָ אֲשֶׁר תַּעֲשֶׂה בּוֹ אֶת הָאֹתֹת: וּבְמֹפְתִים זה הַדָּם כְּמָה שֶׁנֶּאֱמַר וְנָתַתִּי מוֹפְתִים בַּשָּׁמַיִם וּבָאָרֶץ: דָּ״ם. וָאֵ״שׁ. וְתִימְרוֹ״ת עָשָׁ״ן:

דָּבָר אַחֵר. בְּיָד חֲזָקָה שְׁתַּיִם. וּבִזְרֹעַ נְטוּיָה שְׁתַּיִם. וּבְמֹרָא גָּדֹל שְׁתַּיִם. וּבְאֹתוֹת שְׁתַּיִם. וּבְמוֹפְתִים שְׁתַּיִם. אֵלּוּ עֶשֶׂר מַכּוֹת שֶׁהֵבִיא הַקָּדוֹשׁ בָּרוּךְ הוּא עַל הַמִּצְרִיִּים בְּמִצְרַיִם. וְאֵלּוּ הֵן.

דָּם. צְפַרְדֵּעַ. כִּנִּים. עָרוֹב. דֶּבֶר. שְׁחִין. בָּרָד. אַרְבֶּה. חֹשֶׁךְ. מַכַּת בְּכוֹרוֹת: רַבִּי יְהוּדָה הָיָה נוֹתֵן בָּהֶם סִימָנִים. דְּצַ״ךְ. עֲדַ״שׁ. בְּאַחַ״ב:

רַבִּי יוֹסֵי הַגְּלִילִי אוֹמֵר מִנַּיִן אַתָּה אוֹמֵר שֶׁלָּקוּ הַמִּצְרִיִּים בְּמִצְרַיִם עֶשֶׂר מַכּוֹת וְעַל הַיָּם לָקוּ חֲמִשִּׁים מַכּוֹת. בְּמִצְרַיִם מָה הוּא אוֹמֵר וַיֹּאמְרוּ הַחַרְטֻמִּים אֶל פַּרְעֹה אֶצְבַּע אֱלֹהִים הִוא. וְעַל הַיָּם מָה הוּא אוֹמֵר וַיַּרְא יִשְׂרָאֵל אֶת הַיָּד הַגְּדֹלָה אֲשֶׁר עָשָׂה יְיָ בְּמִצְרַיִם וַיִּירְאוּ הָעָם אֶת יְיָ וַיַּאֲמִינוּ בַּיְיָ וּבְמֹשֶׁה עַבְדּוֹ: כַּמָּה לָקוּ בְאֶצְבַּע עֶשֶׂר מַכּוֹת אֱמוֹר מֵעַתָּה בְּמִצְרַיִם לָקוּ עֶשֶׂר מַכּוֹת וְעַל הַיָּם לָקוּ חֲמִשִּׁים מַכּוֹת: רַבִּי אֱלִיעֶזֶר אוֹמֵר מִנַּיִן שֶׁכָּל מַכָּה וּמַכָּה שֶׁהֵבִיא הַקָּדוֹשׁ בָּרוּךְ הוּא עַל הַמִּצְרִיִּים בְּמִצְרַיִם הָיְתָה שֶׁל אַרְבַּע מַכּוֹת, שֶׁנֶּאֱמַר יְשַׁלַּח בָּם חֲרוֹן אַפּוֹ עֶבְרָה וָזַעַם וְצָרָה מִשְׁלַחַת מַלְאֲכֵי רָעִים:

מַה נִּשְׁתַּנָּה הַלַּיְלָה הַזֶּה מִכָּל הַלֵּילוֹת. עֲבָבְ‏ ווֹילוּנוּ אֲנוּ אוֹכְלִין חָמֵץ וּמַצָּה. וְהַלַּיְלָה הַזֶּה כֻּוילוֹ מַצָּה: שֶׁבְּכָל הַלֵּילוֹת אָנוּ אוֹכְלִין שְׁאָר יְרָקוֹת. הַלַּיְלָה הַזֶּה מָרוֹר: שֶׁבְּכָל הַלֵּילוֹת אֵין אָנוּ מַטְבִּילִין אֲפִילוּ פַּעַם אֶחָת. הַלַּיְלָה הַזֶּה שְׁתֵּי פְעָמִים: שֶׁבְּכָל הַלֵּילוֹת אָנוּ אוֹכְלִיס בֵּין יוֹשְׁבִין וּבֵין מְסֻבִּין. הַלַּיְלָה הַזֶּה כֻּלָּנוּ מְסֻבִּין:

עֲבָדִים הָיִינוּ לְפַרְעֹה בְּמִצְרָיִם. וַיּוֹצִיאֵנוּ יְיָ אֱלֹהֵינוּ מִשָּׁם בְּיָד חֲזָקָה וּבִזְרֹעַ נְטוּיָה. וְאִלּוּ לֹא הוֹצִיא הַקָּדוֹשׁ בָּרוּךְ הוּא אֶת אֲבוֹתֵינוּ מִמִּצְרַיִם. הֲרֵי אָנוּ וּבָנֵינוּ וּבְנֵי בָנֵינוּ מְשֻׁעְבָּדִים הָיִינוּ לְפַרְעֹה בְּמִצְרָיִם. וַאֲפִילוּ כֻּלָּנוּ חֲכָמִים כֻּלָּנוּ נְבוֹנִים כֻּלָּנוּ זְקֵנִים כֻּלָּנוּ יוֹדְעִים אֶת הַתּוֹרָה מִצְוָה עָלֵינוּ לְסַפֵּר בִּיצִיאַת מִצְרָיִם. וְכָל הַמַּרְבֶּה לְסַפֵּר בִּיצִיאַת מִצְרַיִם הֲרֵי זֶה מְשֻׁבָּח:

מַעֲשֶׂה בְּרַבִּי אֱלִיעֶזֶר וְרַבִּי יְהוֹשֻׁעַ וְרַבִּי אֶלְעָזָר בֶּן עֲזַרְיָה וְרַבִּי עֲקִיבָא וְרַבִּי טַרְפוֹן. שֶׁהָיוּ מְסֻבִּין בִּבְנֵי בְרַק וְהָיוּ מְסַפְּרִים בִּיצִיאַת מִצְרַיִם כָּל אוֹתוֹ הַלַּיְלָה עַד שֶׁבָּאוּ תַלְמִידֵיהֶם וְאָמְרוּ לָהֶם. רַבּוֹתֵינוּ הִגִּיעַ זְמַן קְרִיאַת שְׁמַע שֶׁל שַׁחֲרִית:

אָמַר רַבִּי אֶלְעָזָר בֶּן עֲזַרְיָה הֲרֵי אֲנִי כְּבֶן שִׁבְעִים שָׁנָה וְלֹא זָכִיתִי שֶׁתֵּאָמֵר יְצִיאַת מִצְרַיִם בַּלֵּילוֹת עַד שֶׁדְּרָשָׁהּ בֶּן זוֹמָא שֶׁנֶּאֱמַר לְמַעַן תִּזְכֹּר אֶת יוֹם צֵאתְךָ מֵאֶרֶץ מִצְרַיִם כֹּל יְמֵי חַיֶּיךָ. יְמֵי חַיֶּיךָ הַיָּמִים. כָּל יְמֵי חַיֶּיךָ הַלֵּילוֹת. וַחֲכָמִים אוֹמְרִים יְמֵי חַיֶּיךָ הָעוֹלָם הַזֶּה. כָּל יְמֵי חַיֶּיךָ לְהָבִיא לִימוֹת הַמָּשִׁיחַ:

בָּרוּךְ הַמָּקוֹם. בָּרוּךְ הוּא. בָּרוּךְ שֶׁנָּתַן תּוֹרָה לְעַמּוֹ יִשְׂרָאֵל. בָּרוּךְ הוּא. כְּנֶגֶד אַרְבָּעָה בָנִים דִּבְּרָה תוֹרָה.

אֶחָד חָכָם, וְאֶחָד רָשָׁע, וְאֶחָד תָּם, וְאֶחָד שֶׁאֵינוֹ יוֹדֵעַ לִשְׁאוֹל:

חָכָם מָה הוּא אוֹמֵר. מָה הָעֵדוֹת וְהַחֻקִּים וְהַמִּשְׁפָּטִים אֲשֶׁר צִוָּה יְיָ אֱלֹהֵינוּ אֶתְכֶם. אַף אַתָּה אֱמָר לוֹ כְּהִלְכוֹת הַפֶּסַח אֵין מַפְטִירִין אַחַר הַפֶּסַח אֲפִיקוֹמָן:

רָשָׁע מָה הוּא אוֹמֵר. מָה הָעֲבוֹדָה הַזֹּאת לָכֶם. לָכֶם וְלֹא לוֹ. וּלְפִי שֶׁהוֹצִיא אֶת עַצְמוֹ מִן הַכְּלָל כָּפַר בָּעִקָּר. וְאַף אַתָּה הַקְהֵה אֶת שִׁנָּיו וֶאֱמָר לוֹ בַּעֲבוּר זֶה עָשָׂה יְיָ לִי בְּצֵאתִי מִמִּצְרָיִם: לִי וְלֹא לוֹ. אִלּוּ הָיָה שָׁם לֹא הָיָה נִגְאָל:

תָּם מָה הוּא אוֹמֵר. מַה זֹּאת. וְאָמַרְתָּ אֵלָיו בְּחֹזֶק יָד הוֹצִיאָנוּ יְיָ מִמִּצְרַיִם מִבֵּית עֲבָדִים:

וְשֶׁאֵינוֹ יוֹדֵעַ לִשְׁאוֹל אַתְּ פְּתַח לוֹ. שֶׁנֶּאֱמַר וְהִגַּדְתָּ לְבִנְךָ בַּיּוֹם הַהוּא לֵאמֹר בַּעֲבוּר זֶה עָשָׂה יְיָ לִי בְּצֵאתִי מִמִּצְרָיִם:

יָכוֹל מֵרֹאשׁ חֹדֶשׁ תַּלְמוּד לוֹמַר בַּיּוֹם הַהוּא. אִי בַּיּוֹם הַהוּא יָכוֹל מִבְּעוֹד יוֹם. תַּלְמוּד לוֹמַר בַּעֲבוּר זֶה. בַּעֲבוּר זֶה לֹא אָמַרְתִּי אֶלָּא בְּשָׁעָה שֶׁיֵּשׁ מַצָּה וּמָרוֹר מֻנָּחִים לְפָנֶיךָ:

מִתְּחִלָּה עוֹבְדֵי כּוֹכָבִים הָיוּ אֲבוֹתֵינוּ וְעַכְשָׁו קֵרְבָנוּ הַמָּקוֹם לַעֲבוֹדָתוֹ. שֶׁנֶּאֱמַר וַיֹּאמֶר יְהוֹשֻׁעַ אֶל כָּל הָעָם כֹּה אָמַר יְיָ אֱלֹהֵי יִשְׂרָאֵל בְּעֵבֶר הַנָּהָר יָשְׁבוּ אֲבוֹתֵיכֶם מֵעוֹלָם תֶּרַח אֲבִי אַבְרָהָם וַאֲבִי נָחוֹר וַיַּעַבְדוּ אֱלֹהִים אֲחֵרִים: וָאֶקַּח אֶת אֲבִיכֶם אֶת אַבְרָהָם מֵעֵבֶר הַנָּהָר וָאוֹלֵךְ אוֹתוֹ בְּכָל אֶרֶץ כְּנָעַן וָאַרְבֶּה אֶת זַרְעוֹ וָאֶתֵּן לוֹ אֶת יִצְחָק: וָאֶתֵּן לְיִצְחָק אֶת יַעֲקֹב וְאֶת עֵשָׂו וָאֶתֵּן לְעֵשָׂו אֶת הַר שֵׂעִיר לָרֶשֶׁת אוֹתוֹ וְיַעֲקֹב וּבָנָיו יָרְדוּ מִצְרָיִם:

ברוך שומר הבטחתו לישראל. ברוך הוא שהקדוש ברוך הוא חשב את הקץ לעשות כמה שאמר לאברהם אבינו בברית בין הבתרים שנאמר ויאמר לאברם ידע תדע כי גר יהיה זרעך בארץ לא להם ועבדום וענו אתם ארבע מאות שנה: וגם את הגוי אשר יעבדו דן אנכי ואחרי כן יצאו ברכש גדול:

והיא שעמדה לאבותינו ולנו. שלא אחד בלבד עמד עלינו לכלותינו. אלא שבכל דור ודור עומדים עלינו לכלותינו. והקדוש ברוך הוא מצילנו מידם:

צא ולמד מה בקש לבן הארמי לעשות ליעקב אבינו שפרעה לא גזר אלא על הזכרים ולבן בקש לעקור את הכל שנאמר ארמי אבד אבי וירד מצרימה ויגר שם במתי מעט ויהי שם לגוי גדול עצום ורב: וירד מצרימה אנוס על פי הדבור. ויגר שם מלמד שלא ירד יעקב אבינו להשתקע במצרים אלא לגור שם. שנאמר ויאמרו אל פרעה לגור בארץ באנו כי אין מרעה לצאן אשר לעבדיך כי כבד הרעב בארץ כנען ועתה ישבו נא עבדיך בארץ גשן:

במתי מעט כמה שנאמר בשבעים נפש ירדו אבותיך מצרימה ועתה שמך יי אלהיך ככוכבי השמים לרוב: ויהי שם לגוי מלמד שהיו ישראל מצינים שם: גדול עצום. כמה שנאמר ובני ישראל פרו וישרצו וירבו ויעצמו במאד מאד ותמלא הארץ אתם:

ורב כמה שנאמר רבבה כצמח השדה נתתיך ותרבי ותגדלי ותבואי בעדי עדיים שדים נכנו ושערך צמח ואת ערום ועריה: ואעבור עליך ואראך מתבוססת בדמיך ואומר לך בדמיך חיי ואומר לך בדמיך חיי:

וַיָּרֵעוּ אוֹתָנוּ הַמִּצְרִים וַיְעַנּוּנוּ וַיִּתְּנוּ עָלֵינוּ עֲבֹדָה קָשָׁה.

וַיָּרֵעוּ אוֹתָנוּ הַמִּצְרִים כְּמָה שֶׁנֶּאֱמַר הָבָה נִתְחַכְּמָה לוֹ פֶּן יִרְבֶּה וְהָיָה כִּי תִקְרֶאנָה מִלְחָמָה וְנוֹסַף גַּם הוּא עַל שֹׂנְאֵינוּ וְנִלְחַם בָּנוּ וְעָלָה מִן הָאָרֶץ:

וַיְעַנּוּנוּ כְּמָה שֶׁנֶּאֱמַר וַיָּשִׂימוּ עָלָיו שָׂרֵי מִסִּים לְמַעַן עַנֹּתוֹ בְּסִבְלוֹתָם וַיִּבֶן עָרֵי מִסְכְּנוֹת לְפַרְעֹה אֶת פִּתֹם וְאֶת רַעַמְסֵס: וַיִּתְּנוּ עָלֵינוּ עֲבֹדָה קָשָׁה כְּמָה שֶׁנֶּאֱמַר וַיַּעֲבִדוּ מִצְרַיִם אֶת בְּנֵי יִשְׂרָאֵל בְּפָרֶךְ.

וַנִּצְעַק אֶל יְיָ אֱלֹהֵי אֲבוֹתֵינוּ וַיִּשְׁמַע יְיָ אֶת קֹלֵנוּ וַיַּרְא אֶת עָנְיֵנוּ וְאֶת עֲמָלֵנוּ וְאֶת לַחֲצֵנוּ: וַנִּצְעַק אֶל יְיָ אֱלֹהֵי אֲבוֹתֵינוּ כְּמָה שֶׁנֶּאֱמַר וַיְהִי בַיָּמִים הָרַבִּים הָהֵם וַיָּמָת מֶלֶךְ מִצְרַיִם וַיֵּאָנְחוּ בְנֵי יִשְׂרָאֵל מִן הָעֲבֹדָה וַיִּזְעָקוּ וַתַּעַל שַׁוְעָתָם אֶל הָאֱלֹהִים מִן הָעֲבֹדָה: וַיִּשְׁמַע יְיָ אֶת קֹלֵנוּ כְּמָה שֶׁנֶּאֱמַר וַיִּשְׁמַע אֱלֹהִים אֶת נַאֲקָתָם וַיִּזְכֹּר אֱלֹהִים אֶת בְּרִיתוֹ אֶת אַבְרָהָם אֶת יִצְחָק וְאֶת יַעֲקֹב: וַיַּרְא אֶת עָנְיֵנוּ זוֹ פְּרִישׁוּת דֶּרֶךְ אֶרֶץ כְּמָה שֶׁנֶּאֱמַר וַיַּרְא אֱלֹהִים אֶת בְּנֵי יִשְׂרָאֵל וַיֵּדַע אֱלֹהִים: וְאֶת עֲמָלֵנוּ אֵלּוּ הַבָּנִים כְּמָה שֶׁנֶּאֱמַר כָּל הַבֵּן הַיִּלּוֹד הַיְאֹרָה תַּשְׁלִיכֻהוּ וְכָל הַבַּת תְּחַיּוּן: וְאֶת לַחֲצֵנוּ זוֹ הַדְּחַק כְּמָה שֶׁנֶּאֱמַר וְגַם רָאִיתִי אֶת הַלַּחַץ אֲשֶׁר מִצְרַיִם לֹחֲצִים אֹתָם: וַיּוֹצִיאֵנוּ יְיָ מִמִּצְרַיִם בְּיָד חֲזָקָה וּבִזְרֹעַ נְטוּיָה וּבְמוֹרָא גָּדוֹל וּבְאֹתוֹת וּבְמֹפְתִים: וַיּוֹצִיאֵנוּ יְיָ מִמִּצְרַיִם לֹא עַל יְדֵי מַלְאָךְ וְלֹא עַל יְדֵי שָׂרָף וְלֹא עַל יְדֵי שָׁלִיחַ: אֶלָּא הַקָּדוֹשׁ בָּרוּךְ הוּא בִּכְבוֹדוֹ וּבְעַצְמוֹ. שֶׁנֶּאֱמַר וְעָבַרְתִּי בְאֶרֶץ מִצְרַיִם בַּלַּיְלָה הַזֶּה וְהִכֵּיתִי כָל בְּכוֹר בְּאֶרֶץ מִצְרַיִם מֵאָדָם וְעַד בְּהֵמָה וּבְכָל אֱלֹהֵי מִצְרַיִם אֶעֱשֶׂה שְׁפָטִים אֲנִי יְיָ: וְעָבַרְתִּי בְאֶרֶץ מִצְרַיִם בַּלַּיְלָה הַזֶּה אֲנִי וְלֹא מַלְאָךְ. וְהִכֵּיתִי כָל בְּכוֹר בְּאֶרֶץ מִצְרַיִם אֲנִי וְלֹא שָׂרָף. וּבְכָל אֱלֹהֵי מִצְרַיִם אֶעֱשֶׂה שְׁפָטִים אֲנִי יְיָ אֲנִי הוּא וְלֹא הַשָּׁלִיחַ. אֲנִי יְיָ אֲנִי הוּא וְלֹא אַחֵר:

עברה אחת. וזעם שתים. וצרה שלש. משלחת מלאכי
רעים ארבע. אמור מעתה במצרים לקו ארבעים מכות ועל הים לקו
מאתים מכות:

רבי עקיבא אומר מנין שכל מכה ומכה שהביא
הקדוש ברוך הוא על המצריים במצרים היתה של חמש מכות.
שנאמר ישלח בם חרון אפו עברה וזעם וצרה משלחת
מלאכי רעים: חרון אפו אחת. עברה שתים. וזעם שלש.
וצרה ארבע. משלחת מלאכי רעים חמש. אמור מעתה,
במצרים לקו חמשים מכות. ועל הים לקו חמשים ומאתים מכות:

כמה מעלות טובות למקום עלינו:

אלו הוציאנו ממצרים. ולא עשה בהם שפטים. דיינו:
אלו עשה בהם שפטים. ולא עשה באלהיהם. דיינו:
אלו עשה באלהיהם. ולא הרג את בכוריהם. דיינו:
אלו הרג את בכוריהם. ולא נתן לנו את ממונם. דיינו:
אלו נתן לנו את ממונם. ולא קרע לנו את הים. דיינו:
אלו קרע לנו את הים. ולא העבירנו בתוכו בחרבה. דיינו:
אלו העבירנו בתוכו בחרבה. ולא שקע צרינו בתוכו. דיינו:
אלו שקע צרינו בתוכו. ולא ספק צרכנו במדבר ארבעים שנה
אלו ספק צרכנו במדבר ארבעים שנה. ולא האכילנו את המן. דיינו:
אלו האכילנו את המן. ולא נתן לנו את השבת. דיינו:
אלו נתן לנו את השבת. ולא קרבנו לפני הר סיני. דיינו:
אלו קרבנו לפני הר סיני. ולא נתן לנו את התורה. דיינו:
אלו נתן לנו את התורה. ולא הכניסנו לארץ ישראל. דיינו:
אלו הכניסנו לארץ ישראל. ולא בנה לנו את בית הבחירה. דיינו:

על אחת כמה וכמה טובה כפולה ומכפלת למקום עלינו: שהוציאנו
ממצרים. ועשה בהם שפטים. ועשה באלהיהם והרג את בכוריהם ונתן לנו את
ממונם וקרע לנו את הים והעבירנו בתוכו בחרבה ושקע צרינו בתוכו
וספק צרכנו במדבר ארבעים שנה והאכילנו את המן ונתן לנו את השבת

וקרבנו לפני הר סיני. ונתן לנו את התורה. והכניסנו לארץ
ישראל. ובנה לנו את בית הבחירה לכפר על כל עונותינו:

רבן גמליאל היה אומר כל שלא אמר שלשה דברים
אלו בפסח, לא יצא ידי חובתו ואלו הן פסח, מצה, מרור:

פסח שהיו אבותינו אוכלים בזמן שבית המקדש קים על שום מה
על שום שפסח הקדוש ברוך הוא על בתי אבותינו במצרים
שנאמר ואמרתם זבח פסח הוא לי״י אשר פסח על בתי בני
ישראל במצרים בנגפו את מצרים ואת בתינו הציל ויקד העם וישתחוו:

מצה זו שאנו אוכלים על שום מה. על שום שלא הספיק בצקת
של אבותינו להחמיץ עד שנגלה עליהם מלך מלכי המלכים
הקדוש ברוך הוא וגאלם. שנאמר ויאפו את הבצק אשר הוציאו
ממצרים עגת מצות כי לא חמץ כי גרשו ממצרים
ולא יכלו להתמהמה וגם צדה לא עשו להם:

מרור זה שאנו אוכלים על שום מה על שום שמררו המצרים
את חיי אבותינו במצרים. שנאמר וימררו את חייהם בעבודה
קשה בחמר ובלבנים ובכל עבדה בשדה את כל עבדתם אשר עבדו
בהם בפרך:

בכל דור ודור חיב אדם לראות את עצמו כאלו הוא יצא
ממצרים שנאמר והגדת לבנך ביום ההוא לאמר בעבור זה עשה
י״י לי בצאתי ממצרים: לא את אבותינו בלבד גאל הקדוש
ברוך הוא אלא אף אותנו גאל עמהם שנאמר ואותנו הוציא
משם למען הביא אתנו לתת לנו את הארץ אשר נשבע לאבתינו:

לפיכך אנחנו חיבים להודות להלל לשבח לפאר לרומם
להדר לברך לעלה ולקלס למי שעשה לאבותינו ולנו
את כל הנסים האלו. הוציאנו מעבדות לחרות. מיגון לשמחה.
ומאבל ליום טוב. ומאפלה לאור גדול. ומשעבוד לגאלה.
ונאמר לפניו שירה חדשה הללויה:

הללויה הללו עבדי יי הללו את שם יי: יהי שם יי מבורך
מעתה ועד עולם: ממזרח שמש עד מבואו מהלל שם יי:
רם על כל גוים יי על השמים כבודו: מי כי"י אלהינו
המגביהי לשבת: המשפילי לראות בשמים ובארץ: מקימי
מעפר דל מאשפת ירים אביון: להושיבי עם נדיבים עם
נדיבי עמו: מושיבי עקרת הבית אם הבנים שמחה הללויה:

בצאת ישראל ממצרים בית יעקב מעם לעז: היתה יהודה
לקדשו ישראל ממשלותיו: הים ראה וינס הירדן יסוב
לאחור: ההרים רקדו כאילים גבעות כבני צאן: מה לך הים
כי תנוס הירדן תסב לאחור: מלפני אדון חולי ארץ מלפני
אלוה יעקב: ההפכי הצור אגם מים חלמיש למעינו מים:

ברוך אתה יי אלהינו מלך העולם אשר גאלנו וגאל את
אבותינו ממצרים והגיענו הלילה הזה לאכל בו מצה ומרור
כן יי אלהינו ואלהי אבותינו יגיענו למועדים ולרגלים
אחרים הבאים לקראתנו לשלום שמחים בבנין עירך
וששים בעבודתך. ונאכל שם מן הזבחים ומן הפסחים
(במוצ"ש מן הפסחים ומן הזבחים) אשר יגיע דמם על קיר
מזבחך לרצון. ונודה לך שיר חדש על גאלתנו ועל פדות
נפשנו. ברוך אתה יי גאל ישראל:

(כוס שני) בא"י אמ"ה בורי פרי הגפן:
(רחצה) בא"י אמ"ה אקב"ו וצונו על נטילת ידים:
(מוציא) בא"י אמ"ה המוציא לחם מן הארץ:
בא"י אמ"ה אקב"ו וצונו על אכילת מצה:

(מרור) בא"י אמ"ה אקב"ו וצונו על אכילת מרור:
(כורך) זכר למקדש כהלל. כן עשה הלל בזמן שבית
המקדש קים היה כורך מצה ומרור ואוכל ביחד לקים מה
שנאמר על מצות ומררים יאכלהו:

שלחן עורך: צפון: ברכת המזון: כוס שלישי שפוך
הלל: לא לנו עד סוף

הודו לה׳ כי טוב כי לעולם חסדו;

הודו לאלהי האלהים כי״ הודו לאדני האדנים כי״
לעשה נפלאות גדלות לבדו כי״ לעשה השמים בתבונה כי״
לרוקע הארץ על המים כי״ לעשה אורים גדולים כי״
את השמש לממשלת ביום כי״ את הירח וכוכבים לממשלות בלילה כי״
למכה מצרים בבכוריהם כי״ ויוצא ישראל מתוכם כי״
ביד חזקה ובזרוע נטויה כי״ לגוזר ים סוף לגזרים כי״
והעביר ישראל בתוכו כי״ ונער פרעה וחילו בים סוף כי״
למוליך עמו במדבר כי״ למכה מלכים גדולים כי״
ויהרג מלכים אדירים כי״ לסיחון מלך האמרי כי״
ולעוג מלך הבשן כי״ ונתן ארצם לנחלה כי״
נחלה לישראל עבדו כי״ שבשפלנו זכר לנו כי״
ויפרקנו מצרינו כי״ נותן לחם לכל בשר כי״

הודו לאל השמים כי לעולם חסדו:

נשמת כל [illegible]

כוס רביעי — בא״י א׳מ׳ה׳ בורא פרי הגפן.

בא״י א׳מ׳ה׳ על הגפן ועל פרי הגפן ועל תנובת השדה ועל ארץ חמדה טובה ורחבה שרצית והנחלת לאבותינו לאכול מפריה ולשבוע מטובה. רחם יי׳ אלהינו עלינו ועל ישראל עמך ועל ירושלים עירך ועל ציון משכן כבודך ועל מזבחך ועל היכלך ובנה ירושלים עיר הקדש במהרה בימינו. והעלנו לתוכה ושמחנו בה ונברכך עליה בקדשה ובטהרה: (בשבת: ורצה והחליצנו ביום השבת הזה) ושמחנו ביום חג המצות הזה. כי אתה יי׳ טוב ומטיב לכל ונודה לך על הארץ ועל פרי הגפן.
ברוך אתה יי׳ על הארץ ועל פרי הגפן:

חסל סדור פסח כהלכתו. ככל משפטו וחקתו. כאשר זכינו לסדר אותו. כן נזכה לעשותו: זך שוכן מעונה. קומם קהל עדת מי מנה. בקרוב נהל נטעי כנה. פדוים לציון ברנה: לשנה הבאה בירושלים:

ספירת העומר לליל שני של פסח:

בא״י א׳מ׳ה׳ אקב״ו וצונו על ספירת העומר. היום יום אחד לעומר

Ki lau noé Ki lau joé .

Adir bimlucho, bochur kahadbcho, gedudóf jaumru lau, lecho ulecho, lecho ki lecho, lecho af lecho, lecho adaunoihamlocho, ki lau noé, ki laujoé. Dogul bimlucho, hodur kahalucho, wosikow jaumru lau, lcho ulcho, lcho ki. lcho, lcho af lcho, lcho ad;;hamamlocho, ki lau noë, ki lau joë, sakaj bimlucho, chossin kahalocho, taw serof jaumru lau, lcho ulcho, lcho ki lcho, lcho af lcho, lcho Ad..hamamlocho, ki lau noë, ki lau joë. Jochid bilucho, kabir kahalocho, limudow jaumru lau, lcho ulcho lcho ki lcho lcho af lcho lcho Ad..hamamlocho ki lau noë ki lau joë, muschel bimlucho, nauro kahalocho, swiwow jaumru lau, lcho ulcho lcho ki lcho lcho af lcho, lcho Ad..hamamlocho, ki lau noë, ki lau joë, onow bimlucho paude kahalocho, zadikow jaumru lau, lcho ulcho, lcho ki lcho, lcho af lch lcho Ad..hamamlocho, ki lau noëki lau joë, kodausch bimlucho, rachum ~~kahalocho~~, schinanow jaumru lau. lcho ulcho, lcho ki lcho, lcho af lcho, lcho Ad..hamamlocho, ki lau noë, ki lau joë, Takif bimlucho, taumëch kahalocho, tmimow jaumru lau, lcho ulcho lcho af lcho, lcho Ad.. hamamlocho, ki lau noë, ki lau joë,

Adir hu jiwne weissau bekorauw, bimhero bimhero bejomenu bekorauw ~~el bene el bene bene wesscho bekorauw~~, bochur hu godaul hu dogul hu jiwne;;;;;;;;;;, hodur hu, wossik hu, sakai hu, chossid hu, jiwne....... tahaur hu, jochid hu, kabir hu, lomud hu, melech hu, nauroh hu, ssagiw hu, isus hu, paude hu, zadik hu, jiwne ;;;;;; kodausch hu, rachum hu, schadai hu, takif hu, jiwne ....

Echod mi jaudea, echod ani jaudea, echod elaukenu schebaschomajim uwoorez. Schnajim mi jaudea, schenajim ani jaudea, schne luchaus habris echod etc. Schlauscho mi jaudea, schlauscho ani jaudea, schlauscho obaus schnei ::::

Arba mi jaudein,arba ani jaudea,arba imohaus,schlauscho ::::
Chamischo mi jaudea,chamischo ani jaudea,chamischo chumsche tauro,arba ::
tauroSchischo mi jaudea,schischo ani jaudea,schischo sidre mischno,cham.:
Schiwo mi jaudea,schiwoani jaudea,schiwo jme schabato,schischo::::
Schmauno mi jaudea,schmauno ani jaudea,schmauno jme milo,schiwo::::
Tischo mi jaudea,tischo ani jaudea,tischo jarche ledo,schmauno::::
Asoro mi jaudea,asoro ani jaudea,asoro dibrajo,tischo::::
Achod osor,mi jaudea,achad osor ani jaudea,achad osor kauchwajo,asoro:::
Schnem osor mi jaudea,schnem osor ani jaudea,schnem osor schiwtajo,achad oso
Schlauscho osor mi jaudea,schlauscho osor ani jaudea,schlauscho osor midajo,
snem osor etc.

Chad gadjo, chad gadjo desabin abo bitre susei, chad gadjo, chad gadjo
weosso schunro weochlo le gadjo desabinabo:::::::::::::
weosso chalbo wenoschach leschunro deochlo gadjo:::::::::::
weosso chutro wehiko lechalbo denoschach leschunro:::::::::::::
weosso nuro wessoraf lechutro dehiko lechalbo denoschach leschunroh::::
weosso majo wechowo lenuro dessoraf lechutro dehiko lechalbo denoschach
leschunro
weosso sauro weschosso lemajo dechowo lenuro dessoraf lechutro dehiko
lechalbo denoschach leschunro:::::::::::
weosso haschauched weschochad lessauro deschosso lemajo dechowo lenuro
dessoraf lechutro dehiko lechalbode denoschach leschunro:
weosso malach hamowes weschochad leschauched deschochad lessauro
deschosso lemajo dechowo lenuro dessoraf lechutro dehiko lechalbo::::
Weosso Hakodausch boruch hu weschochat lemalach hamowes deschochad leschauched deschochad lessauro deschosso lemajo dechowo lenuro dessoraf
lechutro dehiko lechalbo denoschach leschunro deochlo legadjo desabin
abo bitre susei chad gadjo chad gadjo.

Edité du Rabbinat du Rabbin LEO ANSBACHER, GURS (France) NISSAN 5701.

....

Der Lichtblick in dieser Zeit,
waren die Freunde, die wir getroffen.

Leo Ansbacher

A notre Ami
Julien Samuel - au
chasseur infatigable des
nourritures supplémentaires

פותח את ידך ומשביע

Vos

Rabbin Ansbacher

Souvenir de Pesach 5701

ב"ה

הגדה של פסח

קדש ורחץ כרפס יחץ מגיד רחצה מוציא מצה
מרור כורך שלחן עורך צפון ברך הלל נרצה

(יום הששי. ויכלו השמים והארץ וכל צבאם: ויכל אלהים ביום השביעי מלאכתו אשר עשה. וישבת ביום השביעי מכל מלאכתו אשר עשה: ויברך אלהים את יום השביעי ויקדש אתו כי בו שבת מכל מלאכתו אשר ברא אלהים לעשות.) ב"א י"י א"מ"ה בורא פרי הגפן:
ב"א י"י א"מ"ה אשר בחר בנו מכל עם ורוממנו מכל לשון וקדשנו במצותיו. ותתן לנו י"י אלהינו באהבה (שבתות למנוחה ו) מועדים לשמחה חגים וזמנים לששון את יום (השבת הזה ואת יום) חג המצות הזה. זמן חרותנו (באהבה) מקרא קדש זכר ליציאת מצרים. כי בנו בחרת ואותנו קדשת מכל העמים (ושבת) ומועדי קדשך (באהבה וברצון) בשמחה ובששון הנחלתנו. ברוך אתה י"י מקדש (השבת ו) ישראל והזמנים: (ב"א י"י א"מ"ה בורא מאורי האש ב"א י"י א"מ"ה המבדיל בין קדש לחול בין אור לחשך בין ישראל לעמים בין יום השביעי לששת ימי המעשה. בין קדשת שבת לקדשת יום טוב הבדלת ואת יום השביעי מששת ימי המעשה קדשת. הבדלת וקדשת את עמך ישראל בקדשתך. ב"א י"י המבדיל בין קדש לקדש:)
ב"א י"י א"מ"ה שהחינו וקימנו והגיענו לזמן הזה:
ב"א י"י א"מ"ה בורא פרי האדמה:

הא לחמא עניא די אכלו אבהתנא בארעא דמצרים. כל דכפין ייתי ויכול. כל דצריך ייתי ויפסח. השתא הכא לשנה הבאה בארעא דישראל. השתא עבדי לשנה הבאה בני חורין:

ביד חזקה זו הדבר כמה שנאמר הנה יד י"י הויה במקנך אשר בשדה בסוסים בחמרים בגמלים בבקר ובצאן דבר כבד מאד: ובזרע נטויה זו החרב. כמה שנאמר וחרבו שלופה בידו נטויה על ירושלים: ובמורא גדל זו גלוי שכינה כמה שנאמר או הנסה אלהים לבוא לקחת לו גוי מקרב גוי במסת באתת ובמופתים ובמלחמה וביד חזקה ובזרוע נטויה ובמוראים גדלים ככל אשר עשה לכם י"י אלהיכם במצרים לעיניך: ובאתות זה המטה. כמה שנאמר ואת המטה הזה תקח בידך אשר תעשה בו את האתת: ובמופתים זה הדם כמה שנאמר ונתתי מופתים בשמים ובארץ: דם. ואש. ותמרות עשן:

דבר אחר. ביד חזקה שתים. ובזרע נטויה שתים. ובמורא גדל שתים. ובאתות שתים. ובמופתים שתים. אלו עשר מכות שהביא הקדוש ברוך הוא על המצרים במצרים. ואלו הן.

דם. צפרדע. כנים. ערוב. דבר. שחין. ברד. ארבה. חשך. מכת בכורות:

רבי יהודה היה נותן בהם סימנים. דצ"ך. עד"ש. באח"ב:

רבי יוסי הגלילי אומר מנין אתה אומר שלקו המצרים במצרים עשר מכות ועל הים לקו חמשים מכות: במצרים מה הוא אומר. ויאמרו החרטמים אל פרעה אצבע אלהים הוא. ועל הים מה הוא אומר. וירא ישראל את היד הגדלה אשר עשה י"י במצרים. וייראו העם את י"י ויאמינו בי"י ובמשה עבדו: כמה לקו באצבע עשר מכות אמור מעתה במצרים לקו עשר מכות ועל הים לקו חמשים מכות: רבי אליעזר אומר מנין שכל מכה ומכה שהביא הקדוש ברוך הוא על המצרים במצרים היתה של ארבע מכות. שנאמר ישלח בם חרון אפו עברה וזעם וצרה משלחת מלאכי רעים:

Father's Haggadah

Rabbi A. Yehoshu'a Zuckerman

Spring 1941. Detention camp.

A year has past since Father was imprisoned behind barbed wire with twelve thousand other Jews.

The Gurs camp is in France, on the Spanish border. The Pyrenees Mountains tower above the camp. Inside the camp, the French – their hearts with the Germans – rule.

And Passover is near...

Father, concerned for the people's needs, is occupied with organizing work and Torah-study classes, the burial society and the clinic, cultural activities and management of the old-age center.

The spiritual leaders among the prisoners, such as Rabbi Leo Ansbacher (of blessed memory), his brother Mordecai and their friend Dr. Pinhas Rothschild endeavor to instill some life and hope among the downtrodden.

About thirty people die daily of disease and starvation.

And Passover is fast approaching...

Rabbi Kappel, authorized by the French Army and the Chief Rabbinate of France, obtained (as recounted in his book) approximately ten thousand kilograms of flour to bake matzot for all those who – by signing a document – were willing to take the risk of giving up their daily, meager bread ration and possibly end up empty-handed.

Passover has almost arrived and there are no Haggadahs...

Father rose to the task. As he related – and as my sister, too, recalls, he used a hard object to inscribe the entire Haggadah in Hebrew letters, except the songs at the end of the Haggadah, which were typed in Latin letters. He then transferred everything onto paper, and, as Rabbi Kappel testifies in his book, he printed thousands of copies in nearby Toulouse.

The Gentiles' evil is unleashed....

We are nearing the horrors of "The Final Solution." As decreed, and on schedule, the French – lackeys of the Nazis – will transfer most of the survivors

eastward to extermination camps in Poland.

But in Gurs in the Spring of 1941 the Jews read the Passover Haggadah, immersing themselves in their historic past, oblivious of what is to happen.

In Man's Present, His Past and His Future

It is said of Moses that before he decided the fate of the Egyptian taskmaster, "He turned this way and that and saw that there was no man, so he struck down the Egyptian." Our sages explain that he looked into the make-up of this man, asking: Does the merit of his forefathers stand him in good stead? Is he destined to raise righteous children? After turning "this way and that"– to the Egyptian's past and to his future – and seeing that there was no "man," he passed judgment. A person lives in a historical continuum, carrying his nation's past within him, linking it to the future. Therefore, he should not be judged solely for his personal actions, since they reflect his people's history. The Jews in the Gurs camp were a reflection of the nation from its early roots and formation.

For the past 3,311 years, since the Exodus from Egypt and the Revelation at Mount Sinai, the Jewish people have been reciting the story of their rebirth year after year. The Passover Haggadah is read and reflected upon in every home, even as it is now, by those imprisoned in detention camps, condemned to extermination. That is the secret of their eternity, their genetic history! A nation's past courses through each and every individual: "For no one shall be banished from Him." (II Samuel 14:14).

The Sons as Builders of History

As written in the Haggadah: "Here the son asks" – he asks his father and his grandfather. History is bequeathed from father to son. The asking is an integral part of our national legacy. Indeed, we see in Jewish law: "If he is alone – he asks the four questions to himself." (Tractate *Pesahim* 116).

Every child knows the Four Questions by heart and asks them eagerly. Each response generates another question because history flows and develops through the unending nation-building of the sons and "The Strength of Israel does not deceive." (1 Samuel 15:29)

Meanwhile, Father is involved with education in the camp. He writes the

Haggadah from memory, as evidenced by some mistakes found in the Gurs Haggadah.

Father, a scholar and God-fearing Jew who recognized his people's holiness and had a love of humanity, was devoted to the public's needs. He was also accepted by the non-Jews in the camp, who admired his dedication. While in charge of the camp's Jewish burial society, he earned the respect of the French-appointed head of the non-Jewish gravediggers. When Father sensed that the Jews were being sent eastward to Poland, this Frenchman helped Father flee (May 1942) by hiding him in a coffin.

Three Types of Heroes: Heroes of Diaspora Horrors; Nation-Building Freedom Fighters; Day to Day Idealists

The supreme courage evident in the preservation of Jewish identity in the concentration and extermination camps requires explanation.

There is the courage of the brave person who struggles to save himself from drowning under the rising waves of evil, and does not despair. And there is the heroism that stems from the powerful determination of a warrior coming to the defense of his nation. Danger does not deter him; he remains steadfast in his decision to be his people's champion. An inner drive, not personal gain, motivates him to risk his life. Even his mother willingly sends him into battle, saying "Go my son. Defend our people and return to us quickly." This is a war for the nation and for the moral future of humanity.

Heroes of Diaspora Horrors

And then there is the courage needed to devote oneself entirely to the preservation of one's identity. This fighter knows his body will be destroyed. He has no hope of returning from this battle; he has nothing to gain materially from the struggle for either his inner soul or his freedom; nor for upholding goodness, integrity, and universal justice. He only knows he must do battle.

This courage is the courage of eternity. It is not the courage of the present and it does not protect the physical body. This is the courage of the very essence of the soul itself – the soul of Israel!

There are two levels within every Jew: The level of history intermingled with the level of the individual; a single soul with many faces. The Jewish nation lives on, but people die – How is this possible? Indeed the 'vertical line' of history, the line standing in its eternity, extends and reveals itself through the 'horizontal lines,' through the millions of individuals existing in each and every generation: The soul dwells in our world in the 'horizontal line' of the body. Some generations consist of ten million Jews and others of twenty million, and all are called 'Israel' after that one common soul. When they die, the soul of the nation penetrates further along the vertical line of history, through the millions of individuals in the next generation continuing that nation's life.

Generations come and go, and each generation has their own distinctive characteristics – but the national soul is immutable. It is eternity, and with its power comes victory. A son of Israel, faced with the imminent destruction of his body, will abandon it willingly to the flames. He is concerned only in safeguarding his Jewish identity and his values. The price of sacrifice notwithstanding, this devotion to national values instills this warrior with enormous power. He is completely dedicated to the future of his nation's soul. Yet, while a soldier fights for his home, risking his life for the national entity, the camps' prisoners are cloaked in the garb of the soul and manifest in eternal values. For them, only spiritual courage exists,

In Gurs, along the border with Spain – the land of the Expulsion – the Nazified French-Catholics engulf the Jews. Those who courageously seek to preserve their Jewish heritage are akin to their brethren who were tied and burned at the stake by the Church's Inquisition for refusing to worship its evil values. Amidst this hell, the camp celebrated the Festival of Freedom. Those reading the Haggadah during that public Seder in 1941 rose above the horrible, hopeless present to connect with their internal reality – the history that radiates the light of justice and integrity, righteousness and love. The Haggadah binds them to the foundations of their national genesis, no less securely than it did their ancestors on the banks of the Nile or the Talmudic scholars studying on the Euphrates. They, their children, and their grandchildren are bound to the Haggadah for all eternity. They understand the message of the Festival of Freedom, a message passed down from generation to generation: "Next Year in Jerusalem Rebuilt!"

Nation-Building Freedom Fighters

The bravery of the Jewish soldiers, the builders of the state, is greater than the wonderful courage of those in the Diaspora who survived because of their ability to anticipate the future. The sons fight for the international Jerusalem, called

'Talpi'ot,' since she is a *tel* (Hebrew for hill) to which all *pi'ot* (Hebrew for mouths or hymns) are directed. They made her into their capital city. They built the house for its inhabitants, the living, breathing body. But only the sons give meaning to the house.

The Haggadah announces: "The Torah speaks of four sons."

The dedication of the Diaspora "fathers" to the heavenly soul of the nation raises them to the status of angels. And the sons, who fight and build the soul's life in the land and in the body, elevate themselves as humans. The fathers speak of an eternity which conceals the present, while the sons are linked to that eternity within the present. Yet the fathers are commanded "You shall tell your son on that day," as well as the more general "And you shall teach your son," for the sons are the ones building the ideals of the vertical line along the horizontal one. The role of the Prophet Elijah who comes to announce that the kingdom of Israel is returning to sovereignty is to link the generations: "He shall reconcile the parents to their children, and the children to their parents"(*Malakhi* 3:24). His goal is to join heaven and earth. The Haggadah does not hold up the banner of spiritual holiness on the same level that it does material holiness which appears on this earth and in nature. Yet denying the material for the sale of the spiritual runs counter to the sanctity the Almighty reveals. The *nazir* (Nazirite) – one who cannot deal with certain aspects of the real world and finds ascetisim the only way to control and escape nature does not mirror the sanctity of the Creator of heaven and earth. The Almighty's holiness embraces both heaven and earth, while the *nazir,* concerned exclusively with his spiritual well being, is considered a sinner.

The courage of the sons is more difficult to achieve because connecting heaven and earth requires being heavenly on earth, loving the Jewish soul within each person, and loving each Jew – even if one has deep ideological conflicts with that individual. In today's State of Israel, 'love of Israel' finds expression among IDF soldiers. Almost everyone above the age of eighteen serves in the army and is prepared to risk life and limb during war, for the sake of the nation and for the sake of that soul which is common to each and every Jew.

Two thousand years ago hatred among Jews caused a rift in the nation, dispersing it to the four corners of the earth. The nation was exiled from its land and wandered across the earth. The courage that was revealed in the Diasporas exposed the depths of our national character and has resulted today in the courage revealed in the nation's struggle for survival and sovereignty in its land. Thus, despite the nation's exile, the Torah promises: "Yet, even then, when they are in the land of their enemies, I will not reject them or spurn them so as to destroy them, annulling My covenant with them: for I am the Lord their God." (Leviticus, 26:44).

About five hundred years later, when it appeared as though God might renege on His promise to His people because of their sins, Samuel prophesized: "Yet, the Strength of Israel will not lie nor change His mind, for He is not a man that He should change His mind." (I Samuel 15:29).

Approximately one thousand years later, the *tana'im* (early Talmudic scholars) inserted the following praise to God into the Haggadah: "Blessed be He who keeps His promise to His nation Israel, blessed be He!" And the author of the Haggadah continues:

> *"It is this (knowledge) that has helped our fathers and ourselves survive:*
> *that not just one nation has risen up to try to destroy us,*
> *but in every generation they rise up against us to try to destroy us;*
> *and the Holy One, blessed be He, rescues us from their hands."*

And all this has continued for more than 3,300 years.

Day-to-Day Idealists

There is a third form of courage, different from the kind required for the war of survival in the Diaspora or in the Land of Israel: the courage which imbues the daily acts of life with joy. The three forms of courage share one essential quality: that same personal characteristic capable of marshalling powerful internal forces and directing them, undiminished, into one's daily life. The person of courage, although possessing powerful creative abilities, does not apply them indiscriminately. He knows how to cultivate them precisely and sensitively without stifling them. This is what is meant when it says in The Ethics of the Fathers (4:1): "Who is mighty? One who subdues his passions." Thus does the Nation of Israel conduct itself in the Diaspora: successfully containing powerful forces and faithfully expressing them in private life, by raising families – even in a detention camp. There, the glowing ember burns slowly, while the people preserve the spark of life. The inner strength of the people in its daily existence demonstrates great courage manifest in their love for one another, in the tenderness and sensitivity of the mother's hug for her baby, and in the lofty impression made by the actions of an idealist. It is important to know: all those who listen to their inner world can become heroes if they learn to faithfully express their powerful aspirations.

It is written: The commandments "were heard from the mouth of the Courageous One (the Lord)" (Talmud: Tractate *Makot*, page 24). Indeed, the Torah's commandments are designed to give practical and precise expression to the supreme ideals raging intensely within our souls; to the outpouring of the Divine within us. The very word *mitzvot* – commandments – is derived from the word 'to join', to connect heaven to earth, but only when the Jewish people dwell in its land.

In our time, the courage of the nation in its land means giving voice to the historical soul through political and economic life, and through the Hebrew language. Perhaps we must complete this task of nationhood before we can achieve the courage that comes from the intensity of national purpose, and which will ultimately imbue deep love of Israel in every aspect of our lives.

From Holocaust to Revival

The Holocaust, with all its horrors, uprooted the Jews from the lands of the Diaspora. It was a transition period between the few pioneers building the land and the millions who will cause the State of Israel to become a reality, and who will return to the Land of Israel. The courage that emerges from the Holocaust is a silent cry of terrible, abominable suffering which attests to the Jewish nation's existence. This is super-human courage, where human choice and Divine Choice in the people of Israel, intermingle. However, man has little choice in determining whether he is a Jew or part of the historical continuum. The Jewish soul of a person is imposed upon him. It is similar to the unrelenting pressure of birth, but in reverse: At Sinai a historical, national soul – the courage of the Eternal – was born to 600,000 Jews, and at Auschwitz that same soul was almost aborted. The existence of the Jewish people is the common link to both these experiences.

Going to the crematoria because of their Judaism reflects the superhuman courage that remained with our people while in exile. The birth of the nation commenced at Sinai and moves inexorably towards its eternal purpose, as evidenced by the resurrection of the "dry bones" – the Jewish people rising out of the cemeteries of the Diaspora. Once the courage of resurrection appears, then the courage of the sons will become manifest.

> *"And He said to me, O mortal, these bones are the whole House of Israel... Prophesy, therefore, and say to them: Thus said the Lord God: I am going to open your graves,... O My people, and bring you to the land of Israel.... I will*

put My breath into you and you shall live again, and I will set you upon your own soil. Then you shall know that I the Lord have spoken and have acted – declares the Lord." (Ezekiel 37:11-14)

Education, the Hope of Generations

Father was an educator. He devoted himself to lifting the spirits of the prisoners with intense artistic activity, such as concerts or theater performances given by musicians and actors among the inmates, activities that he considered important but not essential. Even the crafts shops which sprang up among the fifteen thousand prisoners were refreshing. But he focused most of his attention on teaching values to the young and the old. He would say, "The nation's hope for the future lies in its investment in education." Thus, he viewed the writing of the Passover Haggadah of supreme value, as is stated: "You shall tell your son on that day saying: 'Because of this, God did for me when I went out from Egypt'" (Exodus 13:8). What is "this"? Each son is different, so "according to the son's ability – his father teaches him." As is stated in the Haggadah: "The Torah speaks of four sons."

Education Reveals One's Natural Abilities and Encourages Their Growth Without any Connection to One's Vocational Knowledge or Training

These words emphasize the basic rule of education: Respect for individual differences and development of personal independence. Even King Solomon linked education to the pupil's nature and stages of development: "Train a lad in the way he ought to go, (and) he will not swerve from it even in old age" (Proverbs 22:6). The Vilna Ga'on interprets:

"'In the way' – according to his nature should you teach and guide him.... but when you force him against his nature, he will obey you now out of fear, but afterwards when you no longer control him, he will turn away..."

The individual differences appear in four ways, all of which should be addressed when teaching: There is the wise son, the wicked son, the simple son, and the son who does not know how to ask. All four sons belong to the nation and to its future rebuilding; the Torah used different approaches when dealing with national or individual issues in order to accommodate the nature and personality of each son.

Education is like agriculture: Abundant sun, irrigation and fertilization are required for growth. The goal of education is to assist children to develop according to their abilities and to find their own way in the world. This job is entrusted to the parents, as is stated "And you shall teach your son properly..." People are social beings and can, therefore, learn in groups; in this case individual personalities should be developed by nurturing common and universal characteristics. Education is meant to elevate an individual, not just to teach a profession and to prepare him for life's struggles. Of course, part of one's personality is that same 'vertical line,' that historical nature and Jewish soul inherent in every child. In exile the soul is hidden; it is revealed when we return to our land and revert to our nature, when we are sovereign, speak our own language, study our cultural roots, breathe the air of our own land. Our goal in education is to activate the person's inherent nature: To be good and honest with God and man.

Each child has certain distinctive qualities which, as the child grows, he has the power to direct. However, certain traits stand out already in childhood. Rather than ignore the unique side of each pupil, the educator should direct it. Educational methods should be adjusted to students' individual natures and their national identity, because people have both general and individual aspects to their personality – one should not be sacrificed for the other. At birth, man is different from all other creatures, yet his birth determines his permanent association with a certain group of people. This group affiliation also has an individual form. As we see in Tractate *Derekh Eretz*: "Just as their faces vary, so do their views." This variation is intensified by free will, which allows people to determine their own paths and conduct themselves according to their own personal codes. The Haggadah expresses this well when depicting the four sons.

Three Inclinations in Human Nature: The Religious, The National, and The Humanistic

Divine truth mandates love and respect for all creatures, regardless of their differences. It also establishes the goals of education and the character of our social life. We must respect each child's special personality and help him adapt to the realities of life. In a group setting, various options should be made available in order to develop the individual, national, and universal inclinations of each person in the group. We should not suppress these three natural inclinations, since they often manifest themselves as three societal movements: the religious, the nationalistic, the humanistic. Furthermore, one who does not function within these three parameters will become functionally handicapped. Nevertheless, at times, one's nature may lead him to favor one principle over the other, which, in turn, may lead to the creation of movements or parties, which are legitimate expressions of these three inclinations. A society which stifles any of these human inclinations is destined to disappear.

Nature demands that we obey its rules, already established at the fetus' formation. The difficulty in harmoniously integrating three opposing forces dwelling within one entity lies in limiting the boundaries of each. It is similar to preventing the fatal spread of cancer in a healthy body. An enlightened society in which everyone is educated according to their nature and which does not reject the three inclinations, has no difficulty respecting and appreciating the three forces.

This basic tenet, which underpins the structure of an enlightened society, derives its power from a higher source, one that is above the three forces and without which they cannot exist. That is the sacred ideal known as 'peace.'

Four Sons

אֶחָד חָכָם, וְאֶחָד רָשָׁע, וְאֶחָד תָּם, וְאֶחָד שֶׁאֵינוֹ יוֹדֵעַ לִשְׁאוֹל:

חָכָם מָה הוּא אוֹמֵר. מָה הָעֵדוֹת וְהַחֻקִּים וְהַמִּשְׁפָּטִים אֲשֶׁר צִוָּה יְיָ אֱלֹהֵינוּ אֶתְכֶם. אַף אַתָּה אֱמָר לוֹ כְּהִלְכוֹת הַפֶּסַח אֵין מַפְטִירִין אַחַר הַפֶּסַח אֲפִיקוֹמָן:

רָשָׁע מָה הוּא אוֹמֵר. מָה הָעֲבוֹדָה הַזֹּאת לָכֶם. לָכֶם וְלֹא לוֹ. וּלְפִי שֶׁהוֹצִיא אֶת עַצְמוֹ מִן הַכְּלָל כָּפַר בְּעִקָּר. וְאַף אַתָּה הַקְהֵה אֶת שִׁנָּיו וֶאֱמָר לוֹ בַּעֲבוּר זֶה עָשָׂה יְיָ לִי בְּצֵאתִי מִמִּצְרָיִם: לִי וְלֹא לוֹ. אִלּוּ הָיָה שָׁם לֹא הָיָה נִגְאָל:

תָּם מָה הוּא אוֹמֵר. מַה זֹּאת. וְאָמַרְתָּ אֵלָיו בְּחֹזֶק יָד הוֹצִיאָנוּ יְיָ מִמִּצְרַיִם מִבֵּית עֲבָדִים:

וְשֶׁאֵינוֹ יוֹדֵעַ לִשְׁאוֹל אַתְּ פְּתַח לוֹ. שֶׁנֶּאֱמַר וְהִגַּדְתָּ לְבִנְךָ בַּיּוֹם הַהוּא לֵאמֹר בַּעֲבוּר זֶה עָשָׂה יְיָ לִי בְּצֵאתִי מִמִּצְרָיִם:

The Wicked Son: **Denies the foundation of faith, denies the national identity in his search for freedom.**

The Wise Son: **Uses his inner force of freedom to search for the ways of his people in order to infuse them within his personality.**

The Simple Son: **The treasures of the future are rooted in the innocence of his childhood.**

The Son Who Does Not Know How to Ask: **His unreserved love for all is the source of the other three sons' questions.**

The Seder (Hebrew for 'order') which guides the night, begins with kadesh – sanctification – the *kiddush* (Hebrew for blessing over the wine). This is the appropriate introduction to the education of the four sons and to observing the commandment, 'You shall tell your son.' The Jews in Gurs were sanctified as well. Sanctification separates; it elevates. But it also sparkles, shines, warms, and revives.

On Passover eve 1941, the fourteenth of Nissan, the sun sets, the world gradually becomes fragrant, and the air purifies. This particular Passover eve is special since it coincides with the holy Sabbath. The sharp barbed wire fence cannot prevent its arrival. Death dwells within as the sun sets, but the internal sun rises and shines...

"...And you have given us, God, in love, Shabbat days for rest, appointed times for rejoicing, festivals and seasons for joy; this Shabbat and this Feast of the Matzot, the season of our freedom... Blessed are You, God, who sanctifies the Shabbat and Israel and the festive seasons." Sanctification is the foundation upon which every segment of the living organism called society must be based.

Let us now examine the designations given to the different groups in society.

The Wicked One: Denies the foundation of faith, denies the national identity in his search for freedom

The wicked one is defined as someone who is unwilling to respect society.

"Therefore, because he has excluded himself from the community...." Similarly, our sages deduce from the question this son asks his father: "What does this service mean to you?" that he is actively alienating himself from the nation. "To you," our Sages expound, "but not to himself." He addresses his father by presenting his question as a challenge and as a means of excluding himself from everyone.

This is not a question which indicates his personal lifestyle; it is a declaration which isolates the individual from the communal – "To you" (he says), "but not to him" – he has removed himself from the community! This is tantamount to denying the foundation of our faith, and to cutting oneself off from eternal holiness. If he despises his nation, even if he is leading a religious life, he cannot be considered saintly.

However, the *Ari Hakadosh* (Rabbi Isaac Luria) warns that even if the wicked son wants to be removed from society, we do not have the power to dissolve his relationship with the world, a world which defines him as a person and as a Jew. This concept is exemplified in the Hebrew word *tzibbur* (community). The first letter of this word, *tzaddi,* stands for *tzaddik*, saint; the last letter of this word, resh, stands for *rasha,* wicked. Each person in the community must choose whether he wants to be part of the *tzaddi* or the *resh*. But it is the individual's choice, not the community's. The wicked son is part of the community by virtue of his birth. He must choose whether to express the communal aspects of his personality, or to reject society and thus cut himself off from the linear line of his nation's history.

Woe to the society that has a wicked person at its head, of which it is said "Sin crouches at the door" (Genesis 4:7). The Hebrew word for 'crouches' is *rovetz*, which utilizes the same letters as *tzibbur,* except that the resh is now the first letter, and the *tzadi* is the last letter.

The Ari further teaches us that the acronym for the word *tzibbur* represents its three components: the saintly, the average, and the wicked. The wicked son strives to cut himself off from the community, as opposed to the saint who feels good about things that go well for others, and cannot find good in another's pain. The saint of the Torah is personified in the Haggadah. He utilizes his communal abilities to help others uncover their hidden selves. Such a person is a community's natural leader. The commandment, "You shall love your fellow as yourself" is a natural part of such a person. Like you like him. Without quashing his own individuality, the saint reveals to others the possibility of choosing a multitude of lifestyles. The saint's individuality is not cut off from society but is part of it, as it helps society expose its own power. The saint has to develop his personality – struggle to fulfill his potential – until he emerges as a new being.

The *tana* (author of the Haggadah) was careful to juxtapose the 'wise son' rather than the 'saintly son' against the 'wicked' so that the two words would complement each other, i.e. it is possible to be wise without being saintly, just as it is possible to be wicked and wise. The wise son seeks reasons for everything and searches for the rules governing life. But the wicked son is also curious, asking,

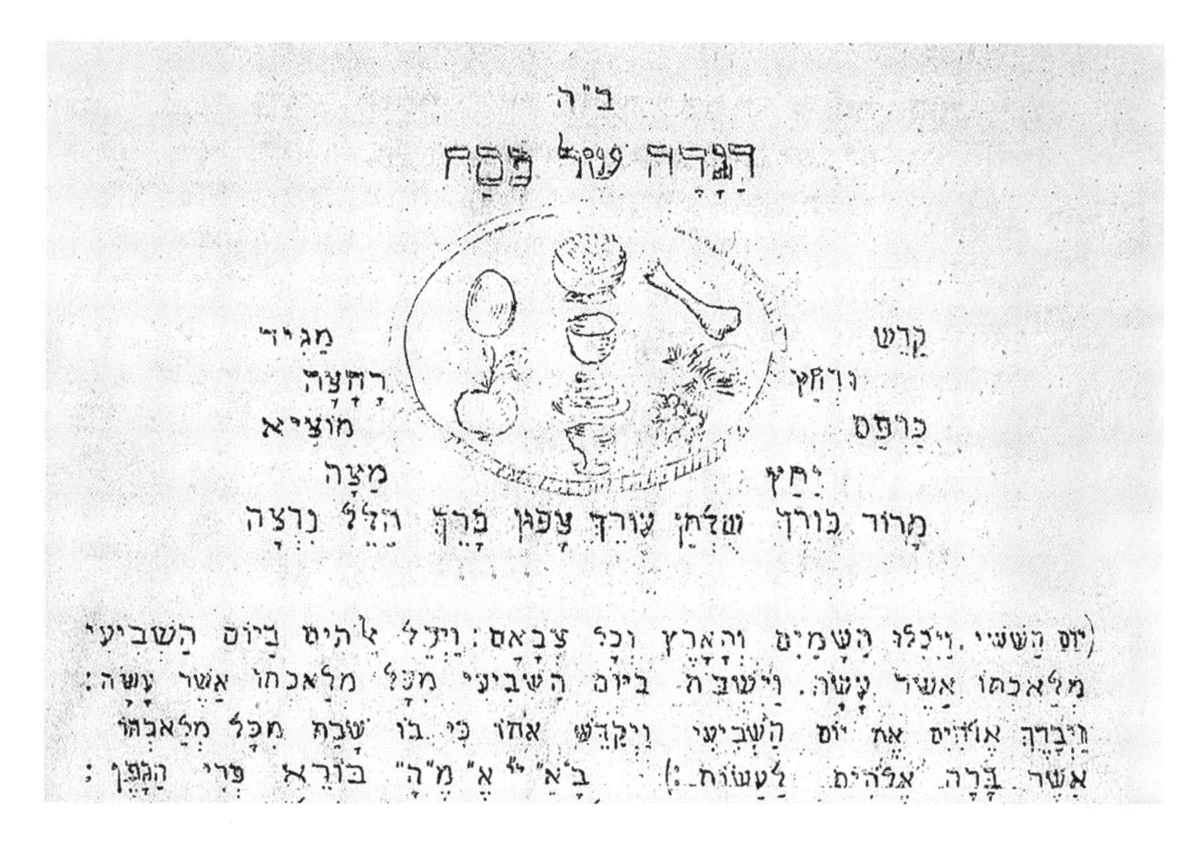

"What is this service?" It is not here that his evil manifests itself. Our rabbis stress that it is in his contempt for community "to you" – and his self-exclusion from the service that we glimpse the evil that lies within.

The Wise Son: Uses his inner force to search for ways to infuse the Jewish people with his personality

Every person's lifestyle is based on how he manifests his love and his connection to his people. Only acts which express the national character of a people are truly natural, healthy and divine. As long as people respect the universal aspects of nation and society, they will be able to reveal these elements in their individual lives.

The designations 'religious' and 'secular' have no place in the Haggadah or in *halakhah* (religious law). We ask: Who is a Jew? And the answer is clear: One whose mother is Jewish! One who is born to his nation, and acts as part of that nation, as revealed in the saintliness of the wise son.

Yet, even the wise son's question, "What are the testimonies, statutes and laws that God has commanded you?" seems to isolate him from the community. What is the difference between the wicked son's "What does this service mean to you?"

and the wise son's "...that God has commanded you?" Why are we told to answer the wise son's question with, "Do then instruct him in the laws of Passover" and the wicked son with, "It is because of this that God did (the miracles) for me when I went out from Egypt."?

The answer lies with the first part of the wise son's question "What are these statutes?" He makes his question relevant to the nation's continuity, so our answer re-enforces his continuity with his people.

However, the rabbi's explain, the wicked son "has excluded himself from the community; he has denied the foundation of our faith..." The answer of the father, "for me, not for him" is echoed in the belief that "Had he been there, he would not have been redeemed." This severance from the eternal-vertical line which finds its expression in the sanctity of the community is a denial of the foundation of our faith, and an impediment to the nourishment that sustains the individual. This individual has no hope for the future even if he observes the commandments and respects the divine service. Such a person's actions may be correct, but by cutting himself off from humanity and from history he renders his actions valueless, and this is a denial of the foundations of the faith. Without a past there is no future to his present. As Maimonides writes: "He who abandons the public path, even if he has committed no sins, but separated himself from the community of Israel... and did not share their troubles... it is as if he is not one of them – he has no part in the world to come." (The Laws of Repentance, 3:11).

The use of the word "you" by the wise son does not indicate exclusion. The wise son knows how to phrase his question in a way that includes him in the roots of the 'vertical line' when he mentions "God"; his question stems from his personal-individual status in relation to the general community. His interest comes from the knowledge that the distance between individual and society is as great as that between heaven and earth. He is asking: "How can I elevate my personality so that I may be included in the community's holiness?" Therefore, "Do then instruct him," in the same vein and with the same purpose in order to nurture his natural inclination. "Do then," in accordance with his character, "instruct him."

These, then, are the two extremes deriving from a person's free will: affiliation with society or withdrawal from it.

We now understand why the saintly son who finds his way towards society is called "wise," while the second son is called "wicked" and not "ignorant." Thus should the father-educator heed the inner feelings of each son, knowing that each is different. This point of view dictates that he respect both the general-historical nature as well as the personal one. With the 'wicked son' what needs to be respected is certainly the general nature, which manifests itself in free will. During the Exodus from Egypt, the nation ascended to its freedom and shattered the yoke of slavery. The secret of freedom lies in the divine image of each person. Human beings, created in the divine image, must liken themselves to God and to His general divineness. Just as God sustains all and plays a role in the life of every living creature and plant, so humans, too, were created in the way that their individual personalities encompass all creatures. It is within the individual's power to express all those hues of life that exist in each one of us.

As part of this universality, people were given the ability to control and direct the rules of nature at will. But the command "They shall rule over the fish of the sea" (Genesis 1:28) is a double-edged sword for humanity: "If they are worthy, they rule; if not, they are subordinate."

The wise son discovers the justice and honesty embedded in the commandment "You shall love your fellow as yourself," and is elevated to a level commensurate with the growth of his personality. Even the wicked son is not just a criminal solely intent upon a life of lawlessness. As an intelligent person, he is curious about the Passover service. His mistake lies in perceiving the historical birth of the Exodus as an obstacle to his personal freedom. His goal of self-fulfillment, of creating a form of independence "What does this service mean to you?" removes him from society, and thus he denies the foundation of our faith. It is up to the father to respect his son's desire for independence and self-fulfillment, to direct him toward constructive use of his intelligence, and, at the same time, to neutralize his biting sarcasm. As the Haggadah says, "You must blunt his teeth." Only within his inner spiritual world will the son find the enormous powers necessary to live up to his potential. This inner world is his entire past, his national legacy that has been funneled into his very being.

The parameters used to define "the wicked son" sheds light on the essence of the saint and the verse in Isaiah "And your people, all of them righteous." As a nation, the People of Israel embody ethics and justice. By upholding these virtues, each righteous individual will perpetuate morality in a world nourished by its holy source. "These are the people of the Lord" (Ezekiel, 36:20), and they must provide a blessing for the world by teaching sacred values and integrity. For the father to fulfill "And you shall teach them properly to your children," he must first alter the mistaken perceptions ingrained in his son and restore him to his people and his land. Then this son's exodus from Egypt and his trek to freedom will commence "You must blunt his teeth and reply to him: 'It is because of this that God did for me when I went out from Egypt'... Had he been there, he would not have been redeemed." The father will teach him how to combine individuality and community through parental nurturing "You shall teach them properly to your children and you shall speak of them while you sit in your home..."

The Simple Son: The treasures of the future are rooted in the innocence of his childhood

The simple son reveals the element of free will given to people of the Exodus. He is at the beginning of his journey in life and still retains the innocence of childhood. He is unaware of the treasure hidden within each person, and still marvels at the wonders around him.

What is it he sees?

The Haggadah gives us a clue: "Why is this night different from all other nights?" Man is comprised of aspirations and the need to expand his horizons. This drive is expressed in the word *adam* (man), which has the same numerical value (45) as the Hebrew word, *mah* (what?). There is something lacking in a person who does not ask questions. Humans, in contrast to all other creatures which are inherently perfect, are perpetually in the process of achieving perfection. Innumerable treasures constantly flow through each individual until he cannot help but discover them. A person does not have to achieve perfection nor should he worry that he is not even close to perfection. But he should regret not having tried hard enough to reach his potential – "The greater the effort, the greater the reward." (Ethics of the Fathers 5:23)

"Man was born to toil" (Job 5:7). Human beings are the only creatures which implement God's infinite revelation. Other creatures discover Him in their unique, limited and unvarying way. The simple son is still connected to his innocence and his wholeness, to the divine treasure that appears at the beginning of his path; he has no flaws, he has not yet left the nest and experienced the vicissitudes of life.

The simple son's intelligence is revealed when he senses the rungs of the ladder whose base is on the ground and whose top is hidden somewhere in the infinite heavens. "Why is this night different from all other nights?" The unique revelation of Passover is that on this Night of God's Protection, the Gates of Hidden Dreams were opened to us, and out poured Divine Wisdom penetrating the hearts of the Jewish nation. "Even the lowest maidservant at (the splitting of) the Red Sea saw visions that Ezekiel son of Buzi and his fellow prophets were not privy to see." Indeed, at that moment, "Even fetuses in their mothers' wombs sang the song of praise."

"Then Moses and the Children of Israel sang this song to God!" This is where the dawn of the Jewish people's wonderful history emerges. From "Then," and just as they did then, will the nation forever "sing" the song of God's appearance before them. The Hebrew is written in the future tense (*yashir* = will sing), as opposed to the past tense (*shar* = sang). It is at this juncture of the Exodus that the simple son asks "What is this?" an obtuse question, but one which calls out for us to hear it.

There is no danger that the wicked son, unappreciative of practical wisdom, will lose the internal innocence which he is not in touch with anyway. He is not connected to, and denies the very existence of his inner self. This detachment from "self" is ultimately what leads him astray. His *mah* ("What is this?") is at once a search for self and a retreat into privacy.

As for the wise son, perhaps it would be better if he knew how to preserve his childhood innocence rather than confine it by using self-limiting logic. However, his devotion to his inner world saves him, since it helps him to utilize the innocence of childhood as an inexhaustible fountain to broaden his horizons. "I accounted to your favor the devotion of your youth... how you followed Me in the wilderness." (Jeremiah 2:2).

Like our matriarch Sarah, the wise son learns to preserve the nation's innocence. "Sarah's lifetime was one hundred years, twenty years, and seven years." (Genesis 23:1). Why was Sarah's age listed in this fashion? As our Sages say: At age one hundred, she retained the innocence of a twenty-year old, and at age twenty she retained the beauty of a seven-year old.

The Son Who Does Not Know How to Ask: His unfettered love for all is the source of the other three sons' questions

With the son who does not know how to ask we have reached the source of the 'vertical line', the stillness found in God's soft silent voice – the source of all questions. At these depths, even the wise son is unable to ask. This last son is totally dedicated to universal ideals without knowing how to apply them to his personal life. His roots are immersed in history; he draws nourishment from his past. His national affiliation beats strongly in his persona, which is devoted to his people and their protection. The "son who does not know how to ask" incorporates the basic innocence of childhood that is found in the "simple son, " and yet has the communal tendency that directs the life of the "wise son." At this exalted level, where the "still, quiet voice" emanates, only the insights and dreams of the great visionaries can function.

"A Song of Ascents. When God brings back those returning to Zion, we will have been like dreamers." (Psalms 126:1). The nation dreams of its redemption during the deep slumber of the Diaspora. And like a sleepwalker, the nation rises, its inner vision propelling it forward, its outstretched hands guiding it to its land. The soul has awakened sufficiently to cry out to its scattered, remote nation, calling its people home. As the children return to their land, the loud call fills them with a power they themselves are not aware of. Since they are so awestruck, they can neither comprehend nor ask, but the joy that accompanies their return pervades their very being. They turn to the nation, to that very Israeliness, that sovereignty, to understand the meaning of their independence. Using the father's response to the son who does not know how to ask, the children plead: "You initiate the dialogue" and provide the opening for us to comprehend the significance of what is happening and show us how to connect to the momentous hour.

And when the inner fires spark the nation, it becomes clear that there is no difference between the wise son, the wicked son and the simple son, for they all realize that they do not even know how to ask. And the heavens, the source of everything, lay open before them.

The Messiah's Donkey: A parable concerning how the Four Sons are the source for all the commandments that sanctify Israel's national soul

Father escaped the camp and joined the underground in its struggle against the Nazis. He took his family and fled with them to the depths of the forest in southern Belgium.

Father's philosophy endures as a soul without a body – without a national body, that is, without a land and without a language. And the sons are those building the land; those who, by their nature, are called upon to be loyal to the land and settle it – not to remove themselves from society-at-large or deny the foundation of their faith. This is not the case with the fathers, whose deeds are private and whose connection to the nation is miraculous. Father's philosophy continues and joins the "vertical line" of Jewish history.

Father told us many stories during our time in the forest. One of them was about the fictitious name our family used in order (among other reasons) to obtain food ration stamps. The name he used was Martin, which was what a donkey was called in that region.

The story of the "Martin" family bears similarities to the stories of later wars fought by their sons. They arise from the memories of the time we were stationed at the Suez Canal during the long months of the Yom Kippur War. Many stories floated in the air during the quiet moments at our encampment. When one soldier was asked by his comrade if he believes that the Messiah is coming, he responded: "I don't see the Messiah coming, but I see his donkey," explaining: "We are the donkey."

As the prophet Zechariah said, "Rejoice greatly, Fair Zion; Raise a shout, Fair Jerusalem! Lo, your king is coming to you. He is victorious, triumphant, yet humble, riding on an ass, on a donkey foaled by a she-ass" (Zechariah 9:9).

Here is the parable of the impure animal, defined by the Torah as neither possessing split hooves nor chewing its cud. And specifically on such an animal must the Messiah ride. At his side will appear the soul of the nation returning to its land, to its national body, and to its sovereignty.

The wicked son's sin in denying the foundation of the faith is in his severing himself from the nation's holiness, for which, according to Maimonides, he loses his place in the 'world to come,' even if he observes the commandments. There is no significance to the commandments without the sanctity of the nation. It must be sovereign in its land, love itself and fully develop its way of life. And this will occur only when it observes the commandments, thereby creating a healthy, robust nation.

It is therefore not possible to speak of the Torah's holy commandments without focusing on the nation. The Kingdom of the Lord – embodied in the renewal of the kingdom of Israel and culminating with the coming of the Messiah – precedes the commandments. It is revealed in the return of the nation to its land and in the resurrection of the dead described by the prophet Ezekiel (Chapter 37) in the vision of the dry bones. The nation precedes the commandments in its very essence, not in a temporal sense. There is no sanctity in individuals, unless they perpetuate the sacred values inherent in the soul of the nation. One must constantly keep in mind that the "horizontal lines" – as expressed by billions of individual Jews – are but a continuation and a realization of the 'vertical' line. Judaism is not a religion but a revelation of the nation's character.

Everything stems from a love of Israel. In the words of the parable: The Messiah arrives riding on a donkey. That is, the sovereignty of the people in its land will materialize, even if its citizens' behavior is unsatisfactory and their actions do not reflect the holiness in their souls. However, their love for their nation is the first step in the Messiah's arrival. This love will elicit the wise son's questions after the era of the simple son and the one who does not know how to ask. But, God forbid that the wise son should think that the whole process begins with him. No questions arise from the silent internal voice, but its murmur emerges from the depths of the nation's soul and revives its sons. All has not yet come to pass, as with the donkey, but from the silent voice bursts forth the pure waters to nurture the innocence of the child. This same perfection will burst forth and become rivers of wisdom and streams of water to irrigate the land.

This reality was forced upon the nation during its birth at Mount Sinai, as one who does not know how to ask, but its implementation is dependent upon the sons' free will. The eternity of the 'vertical line,' revealed in the miraculous survival of the fathers, will become the heritage of the sons. Its actualization in their personal lives depends on choices made by future generations, which will be as varied as those made by the Four Sons of the Torah. And until these choices are made, this inner holiness will remain confined. The Messiah's donkey can never be replaced; it symbolizes the renewal of love for one's people that each soldier holds in his heart.

This is the love of a nation for itself, before it takes its place among the nations and develops its own unique identity. This is the soul of the fathers, encased in the national body which is recovering from two thousand years of exile. Sanctity is concealed only within the body of the nation; only on the nation's back will Israel's sovereignty emerge; only from this sovereignty can the holiness of the commandments endure. "A person who dwells outside the Holy Land is akin to one who has no God " (Tractate *Ketubot*: 110). There is no divine presence without a sovereign nation, without a national body in which Israel's soul can dwell. "He has made me dwell in darkness, like those long dead" (Lamentations 3: 6).

The pioneers of yesteryear and the IDF soldiers of today demonstrate the holiness of their people with endless love. This is the secret of eternity, without which the nation will remain in the grave of exile.

This is the sanctity of the Messiah's donkey which we were commanded to redeem, from whose strength stems our eternity, and without which victory is impossible.

The Revival of Prophecy: The old will be renewed and the new will be sanctified when children and parents are reconciled, inspired by the supreme Holy Spirit which awakens the nation to return to its land

These two levels are noted with the first word of the Seder: *Kadesh* (Sanctify), i.e., the commandment to sanctify the day: "Remember the Sabbath day and keep it holy." This requires explanation. After all, the Sabbath and holidays are sanctified with the setting of the sun, so why do the people have to sanctify the day?

Collective sanctity does not negate the individual's power of choice. It allows people to contribute their own nuances to the community. The first *Kadesh* of the Haggadah embodies the 'vertical line' of Jewish history and is forever imposed upon the people from birth, as exemplified by the way the Sabbath begins every Friday night. It can only be attained by the *Kadesh* of the 'horizontal line' which is manifest through the sons. Missing from the first *Kadesh* is its lack of choice; it is pre-determined and fixed within nature, unable to enhance its eternal source. Therefore, renewal of the sons always stems from the father.

The father is interested in his son's questions, and elicits them on the Seder night by adding and changing the order of the meal, which arouses the son's curiosity. The questions reveal a comprehension of reality that reach beyond the father's innate sanctity, transcending his soul. As Rabbi Kook said, "The old will be renewed and the new will be sanctified." The fathers will sanctify the sons with

בא"י אמ"ה בורא פרי הגפן:
בא"י אמ"ה על הגפן ועל פרי הגפן ועל תנובת השדה ועל ארץ חמדה טובה ורחבה שרצית והנחלת לאבותינו לאכול מפריה ולשבוע מטובה. רחם י"י אלהינו עלינו ועל ישראל עמך ועל ירושלים עירך ועל ציון משכן כבודך ועל מזבחך ועל היכלך ובנה ירושלים עיר הקדש במהרה בימינו. והעלנו לתוכה ושמחנו בה ונברכך עליה בקדושה ובטהרה: (בשבת ורצה והחליצנו ביום השבת הזה) ושמחנו ביום חג המצות הזה. כי אתה י"י טוב ומטיב לכל ונודה לך על הארץ ועל פרי הגפן. ברוך אתה י"י על הארץ ועל פרי הגפן:

חסל סדור פסח כהלכתו. ככל משפטו וחקתו. כאשר זכינו לסדר אותו. כן נזכה לעשותו: זך שוכן מעונה. קומם קהל עדת מי מנה. בקרוב נהל נטעי כנה. פדוים לציון ברנה: לשנה הבאה בירושלים:

ספירת העומר בליל שני של פסח:
בא"י אמ"ה אקב"ו וצונו על ספירת העומר. היום יום אחד לעומר

the power of their historical souls, and the sons will renew the appearance of the eternal source, something which is beyond the power of the fathers' holiness to do.

Everything flows and is magnified with persistent and joyous exaltation.

These are two different forms of holiness: the courage of the fathers, evident in the exile, and that of the sons in the redemption. It is incumbent upon the prophet Elijah to carry out this essential, spiritual task; to first "reconcile parents with children," and only afterwards "children with their parents."

The link between father and son, between history and creation, between a nation and its individuals, strengthens its roots in its own land.

The fathers' power is actualized in their offspring; the roots are strengthened as the sons flourish. The fathers must return to the sons; the fathers' hidden power will be elevated by the sons' choices. Yet the sons cannot find the spiritual elation they seek in their immediate circle. Only a supreme force can restore to their inner souls such a spiritual encounter. The experience will bear fruit via the sap that rises from the roots of the fathers. The sons will flourish and multiply for eternity, but not by drugs or by drink. Only by discovery of the supreme internal soul will the sons be filled with the revelations that bring with them vigor and idealism.

The nationalism of Israel is international, just as the heart belongs to all parts of the human body

The *Kadesh* that opens the Haggadah is the holiness of the sons enhancing that of the fathers. All humanity is included in the commandment for the father to teach his children. The top of that same 'vertical line' reaches the highest heavens, to the God of the spheres and all nations.

Father's Haggadah devotes special attention to the section "Pour forth thy wrath upon the nations that do not recognize You, and upon the kingdoms that do not invoke Your name" (Psalms 79:6-7). This is recited before the *Hallel* section (Songs of Praise), which begins with "Not unto us, God, not unto us, but unto Your name give glory, for the sake of Your kindness and truth!"

Many ask if there is any significance to the fact that Father did not bother to inscribe the complete version of this section, but rather alluded to it with the one word, "Pour." Was this due to a lack of paper, as was the case when he shortened the *Birkat HaMazon* (Grace After The Meal) and the *Hallel* (Songs of Praise), or was there another reason?

The truth is that Father treated this section in a special way. He used to say that all the Nazis should be destroyed. However, he did not want to sink to the level of those creatures by giving full vent to his hatred. If, in order to restore morality and faith in this world, vengeance must be taken against the Nazis, then it should be done, but out of a love for ethical values and ideals.

He was very careful with the words of King David: "Pour forth thy wrath upon the nations that do not recognize You" – only upon those that do not recognize You. "And upon the kingdoms that do not invoke Your name," only those who do not invoke Your name. He was not interested in personal vengeance. As we declare: "Not unto us, God, not unto us, but unto Your name give glory, for the sake of Your kindness and truth!"

Under the influence of Christian culture, Europe sanctioned a slaughter of horrifying cruelty and calculated evil. They said, "Let us make them an extinct nation, and the name of Israel will no longer be heard." Christian culture spawned a monster whose limbs were the nations of Europe, excluding those righteous Gentiles whose integrity guided their behavior. This was a system of kingdoms and nations whose moral bankruptcy led to its suicide, as it says, "For your evil will torment you."

The nation of Israel does not share the belief that these nations feel a sense of humiliation, or are disturbed in any way by having behaved in such a loathsome manner. They have to judge themselves, their fate is in the hands of God, and Israel will march on its path toward revival.

My mother-in-law often tells us that only one thought sustained her throughout her years of suffering in Birkenau-Auschwitz. The one point that provided her with hope was that her little daughter was waiting for her. And, indeed, that little girl was held elsewhere by the Nazis. They met and moved to Israel, which they are now helping to rebuild.

When the belief in Divine unity exists in every creature, love and respect for individual differences will exist, and the desire for unity among all creatures will emerge through mutual understanding which proclaims eternal peace.

This is how Father wanted to proclaim the history of his people. Even as the sons were thrust into the cauldron of reality, he cautioned them against disgracing themselves through hatred of God's creatures. Even the verse, "Pour forth thy

הלל: לא לנו

wrath upon the nations" stems from a love for the Divine presence in creatures. This is the ethical legacy bequeathed to humanity; this is how the struggle for peace is won.

Peace is the base of a pyramid. At its apex is the unity that is the root of all existence – "And You instill life in everyone." The unity of the Creator is the stimulus for peace and is essential for its endurance. The unity spreads through the body of the pyramid, which consists of innumerable creatures. The Creator's presence manifests itself in each and every being, from the smallest insect to the angels on high. The belief in unity brings respect for the differences in everyone and allows us to judge each creature by divine standards. Ethical codes which provide structure for a life of idealism have their source in "You instill life in everyone."

The Torah says, "Behold! I set before you today life and goodness, death and evil...Choose life that you and your offspring will live." (Deuteronomy, 30:15-19).

Performing good deeds means adding life and nurturing another's existence in order to demonstrate the will of the Creator. Every person is obligated by his nature to discover the ideal life. Only when he determines how to express God's plan for him, will his desire be awakened to reveal, through every fiber of his being, his true feelings as they relate to this multifaceted world.

Similarly, the nations are called upon to complement each other without blurring their individual identities. Preserving their differences contributes to mutual completion. This is peace.

Peace does not involve relinquishing truth or ideals; it is neither a renouncement of values nor a dimming of individual or national differences. Peace is the perfection of all details, the integration of all parts of the international and societal body into one unit where each limb – with its own task – is nourished by the Supreme fountain, common to all. This fountain gushes more powerfully when all forces cooperate.

Ultimately, the belief in Supreme unity guarantees this same unity on earth, as well as eternal peace.

"Rejoice greatly, Fair Zion; raise a shout, Fair Jerusalem! Lo, your king is coming to you. He is victorious, triumphant, yet humble, riding on an ass, on a donkey foaled by a she-ass. He shall banish chariots from Ephraim and horses from Jerusalem; the warrior's bow shall be banished. He shall call on the nations to surrender, and his rule shall extend from sea to sea and from river to land's end." (Zechariah 9:9-10)

OHofstätter

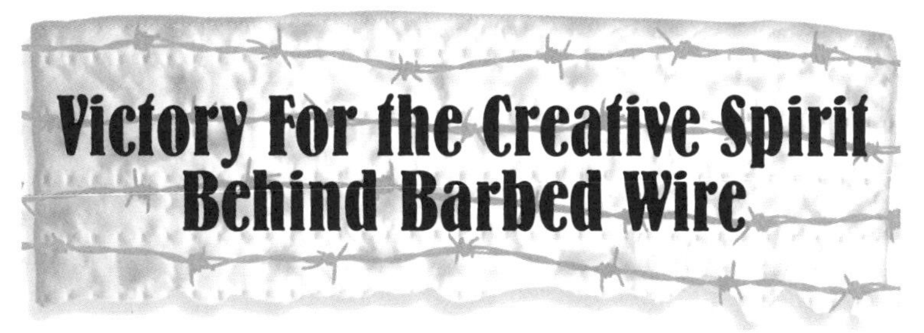
Victory For the Creative Spirit
Behind Barbed Wire

Yehudit Shen-Dar

We produced theater at Gurs,
Would you know what that means?
Behind the barbed wire the world blurred.
And we, eight thousand men and women,
Were miserable and uprooted.
We were living in total wretchedness,
Forgotten, abandoned, orphans,
Packed into gloomy barracks.
The storm of war blew over our heads.
Would you know what that means?
We performed to stay alive,
Nobody knows exactly what that means.
A slice of bread in exchange for Ibsen
An egg for A Midsummer Night's Dream
And perhaps a handful of semolina peppered with contempt.
We rehearsed during freezing nights,
Almost fainting from hunger,
We sang, we danced, we cried, we laughed,
We brought joy, light, and life
To an audience of thousands.
You have no concept of what this means.
We revived thousands of desperate people,
We inspired courage, we rekindled hope and faith.
We endured all of humanity's suffering
But we produced theater...
Think of what that means.

Heine Walfisch, a prisoner at the Gurs camp

Behind the barbed wire fences of the Gurs camp at the foothills of the Pyrenees, an extensive and vibrant cultural enterprise was remarkably created out of thin air. There, thousands of Jews had been robbed of their freedom; there, thousands had been brought against their will from the centers of culture and freedom in France, Belgium or Germany. Among the many who arrived at the camp, in the autumn of 1940, were a considerable number of musicians, actors, cabaret performers, painters and graphic artists. They were the foundation of our cultural enterprise.

How did this come about? Paris of the 1930s was a magnet for anyone involved in the arts. Immigrants from all over Europe filled the studios of the city. Many Jews left their towns in Eastern Europe in order to take part in the European avant-garde. In addition, many refugee German Jewish intellectuals joined the Parisian art scene in 1933 when they escaped from Germany with the Nazis' rise to power. After Nazi forces occupied the art capital of the world, these refugees, lacking French citizenship, were among the first to be thrown into the maelstrom of war and to be sent to detention camps in southern France. It is no wonder, then, that many of the camp's inmates were artists.

"Out of the darkness, the cold, the hunger arose immediately a powerful spiritual resistance which constituted an undeniable victory for the creative spirit." This is how Hanna Schramm describes, in her memoirs, what transpired when they assembled together at Gurs. Every concert, each dance, every theater performance served to dispel, if only for a moment, the feelings of helplessness and loneliness. Here, in the shadow of all this creativity, the individual could feel part of a community sharing a common fate and a singular desire: not to lose the human spirit. Art was but one means of fulfilling this desire, both for the artists as well as the audience.

From early autumn 1940, after a large group arrived from the Saint Cyprien camp which had been washed out in the rains, the cultural activity assumed the tone of an organized enterprise. With the help of the recent arrivals, the Gurs camp quickly developed into a vibrant entity, one with a remarkable abundance of cultural activity, social welfare, and religious services. All this, despite the difficult physical conditions which prevailed in the camp; the cold, the mud, the hunger, and the lack of minimal sanitary facilities. The memoirs of Gurs prisoners bear considerable testimony to the variety and intensity of the cultural enterprise.

During the winter of 1940 one barrack in each block was emptied and transformed into a cultural center, with a platform for the performers and benches for the audience. Lectures were held and classical music performed in these centers.

The designation of space in every block for cultural events indicated the importance with which they were regarded in the camp. Culture became a permanent feature in camp life and served the growing needs of the various artists on one hand, and of the audience, in search of some respite from the bleakness of their routine, on the other.

Music, in particular, assumed special prominence in this cultural world. Concert instruments were brought inside the barbed wire fences from neighboring towns with the assistance of the different welfare organizations which operated in the camp. Wind instruments, string instruments and even pianos were available to the musicians. "There was even a grand piano in one of the assigned culture huts in the women's sector. Everyone started to play it, including those without experience, until it became necessary to set up the 'Abused Piano Guard,'" writes one of the female prisoners in her memoirs. Because so many people longed for a reminder of the life they were forced to abandon, and had the urge to physically touch something that came from "there" – from the world outside the fence – even a grand piano, it became imperative to limit access to it.

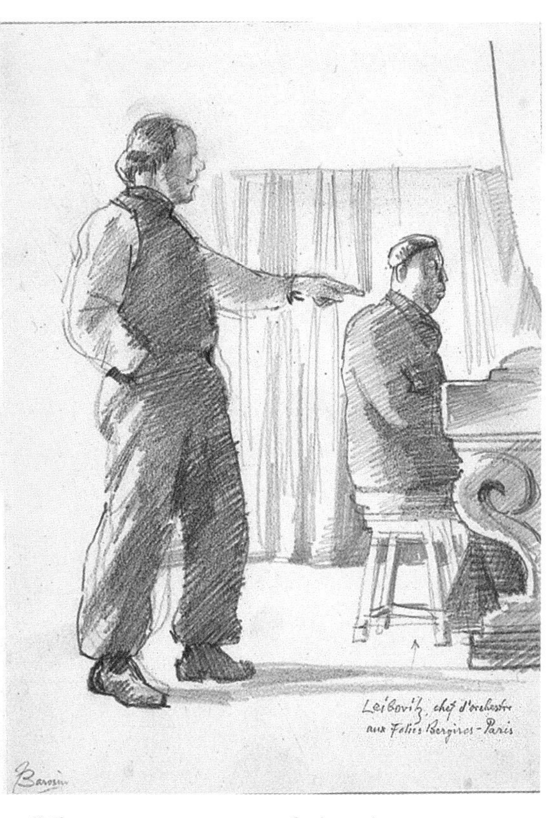

Jacob Barosin
"Leibovitz, Conductor of Folies Bergere orchestra in Paris" Gurs

Pencil on paper,
18 x 25 cm
Collection of
Yad Vashem Art Museum
Donated by the artist

It is clear from written material that everyone in the camp contributed to its cultural life, not just the professionals among the prisoners. The "Menorah" girls, with the help of the camp's artists, prepared a show of songs in Yiddish and Hebrew. According to Rabbi Yehudah Ansbacher: "They sang before three hundred people, who were moved to tears. At my request, the girls continued to perform for a few weeks before the elderly, the weak, the dying, thus providing some cheer throughout the camp." The conductor of the camp's philharmonic orchestra had some musical scores which had been brought in, and the sounds of classical music could be heard several times a week from the cultural centers set up in the various blocks. The camp included some well-known musicians such as Fritz Brunner, the first violinist of the Vienna Orchestra, and Hans Ebbecke, the organist at the

Strasbourg Cathedral, who organized a camp choir from among the professional singers. Concert tickets were in great demand and were sold to inmates for a nominal sum. This fee went toward mutual aid and rental of additional instruments.

The routine of an idle, purposeless life was broken several evenings each week. A variety of shows were staged for the prisoners' relief, including theater and cabaret performances written by the inmates. They were presented on an improvised stage with entertaining sets designed by the two camp artists, Kurt Loew and Karl Bodek. Hanna Schramm writes in her memoirs: "They drew the posters and the invitations. They were also in great demand to produce greeting cards for special occasions, and requests had to be made several weeks in advance in order to be filled on time." This is further evidence that despite the constraints of time and place, amateur and professional artists played an important role in the prisoners' lives. From the various prisoner archives it is clear that there were many fine art professionals among the Gurs inhabitants. There was such an outpouring of creativity that an exhibit of paintings, sculpture, and graphic art was held in the spring of 1941. Participants were very carefully chosen by a panel of judges, and the different relief organizations in the camp supplied the materials; fabrics, brushes, paints, and paper. The exhibit took place in one of the cultural barracks on the men's side of the camp; temporary partitions were added to the available wall space in order to display all the works. The camp experience was evident in all the paintings.

In the summer of 1941 there was another, expanded exhibition, which included more artists and art categories. Besides the many professional, renowned artists who were at the camp, including Osias Hofstatter, Karl Schwesig, Leo Breuer, and Kolos-Vari, among others, there was a large number of amateur artists who participated in this exhibition. They designed different items which decorated the barracks, making them more livable, such as lamps, wood-framed mirrors, jewelry, and colored buttons. This exhibit, even wider in scope than that of its predecessor, was held in the cultural barracks of three different blocks and attracted buyers from the surrounding villages.

The paintings and drawings interspersed throughout this book and accompanying the facsimiles of the Gurs Haggadah, Passover 5701 (1941) afford the readers a glimpse into the world of art that was created in the camp. The reality of Gurs, with all its misery, was portrayed with surprising candor, despite the censoring eyes of the authorities. The fact that many artists chose to depict the camp existence in austere fashion, in monochromatic black and white, was not

Leo Breuer
Gurs Camp, 1941

Watercolor on paper,
22 x 30 cm
Collection of
Yad Vashem Art Museum

due to a lack of paints, but was rather meant to accurately reflect their personal perception of the world of Gurs as a colorless, black and white existence.

Only the snow-capped Pyrenees, emerging over the horizon in the paintings by Leo Breuer, Schleifer, Hofstatter, Barosin, and Berkefeld, allude to another, more beautiful and glorious existence. Nature provides the only light and color in a world that is all gray. Yet that nature, despite its proximity, is completely out of the reach of those inside the camp. The barbed wire fence which "stars" so prominently in the paintings by Breuer, Schleifer, Barosin, Kolos-Vari, and Hofstatter is the physical barrier that unmistakably separates the inside of the camp from the outside, dividing between those with freedom of movement and those deprived of all freedom. All that was left for those fated to be on the inside was the solace they found among their fellow prisoners; anonymous figures wandering in the mud around the camp barracks. The heavy brown, muddy earth appears in all the drawings; the same mud that left its indelible mark on the prisoners' memories.

Passover 5701 was filled with symbolism. Rabbi Yehudah Leo Ansbacher arranged the production of a Haggadah for the thousands who wanted to celebrate the holiday and conduct a religiously correct *Seder*. He was assisted by Aryeh Zuckerman, who wrote the Hebrew text from memory, on stencils. This technique facilitated the printing of the Haggadah in sufficient quantity for everyone to participate. The starkness of the Haggadah and its lack of illustrated text reflect the difficulties under which it was published. The original watercolor painting was added only to "special" editions, and stands in sharp contrast to the modest design of the text.

The Passover scene painted by Fritz Schleifer (see page 54) in which a large gathering of prisoners looks up at their leader, evokes the image of the revelation at Mt. Sinai. Rabbi Leo Ansbacher is delivering his sermon standing at the top of a hill, elevated behind a prayer platform decorated with the Star of David. The artist's perspective makes it appear as though the hill is even higher than the peaks of the Pyrenees in the background. Rabbi Ansbacher's position atop the hill and the diminution of the barbed wire fence behind him are intended to provide concrete expression to the sense of spiritual loftiness of the event. There is no doubt that the artist portrays Rabbi Ansbacher as an exalted spiritual leader, similar to Moses at Sinai. It is conceivable that the artist also meant to convey the people's yearning to believe that their present-day spiritual leader, like Moses of Old, would yet take them from slavery to freedom.

There is an interesting epilogue to the Haggadah of Gurs. The prisoners were aware that the Haggadah had been sent to friends and family outside the camp. These copies included illustrations depicting the Gurs camp, with the Pyrenees Mountains in the background. The small pictures, each about the size of a stamp, were drawn by Karl Schwesig, a non-Jewish artist who was imprisoned at Gurs for his membership in the Communist party. The pictures were designed to draw the attention of the French to the atrocious conditions in the camp.

Schwesig relates in his memoirs that sheets of French stamps had a white border, what collectors call "selvedge." Schwesig utilized this white space for his illustrations, which were an instant success among the inmates, who began to collect them. He took a "tiny" fee from his customers and became a well-to-do prisoner compared to his impoverished peers. The original pictures are in the archives of the Leo Baeck Institute in New York. Because the pictures were attached to the stamps they were not "discovered" by the camp authorities.

At a later date, a letter written by the camp commander to his superiors was found in which he claims to understand the Passover symbols, particularly the significance of freedom in the story of the Exodus from Egypt. Therefore, he adds, there is some propaganda inherent in the publication of the Haggadah, for which those involved should be punished.

The artist Fritz Schleifer was among those deported to Drancy in August 1942. Two months later he was killed at Auschwitz. Fate dictated that two of his works become part of the collection in the Art Museum of Yad Vashem. One is a picture of the Passover prayer service in 5701 (1941), and the other is a view of the Jewish cemetery near the camp; he himself was destined to find neither freedom in life, nor a grave after death.

There is another painting by Fritz Schleifer in the archives of the *Centre de Documentation Juive Contemporaine* (Documentation Center for Contemporary Judaism) in Paris. A Jewish holiday is also the theme of this picture, which describes the interior of one of the camp's synagogues and is entitled: "Gurs Camp, Synagogue, Block F, *Rosh Hashana* 5702 (1941)."

Fear and terror gripped Gurs Camp with the arrival of the Black Shirts. Artistic expression could no longer be considered. After the first transports, Brunner and Leval performed concerts only of somber music and the singers sang only upon the order of the camp commander. The muses at Gurs were silenced in 1942.

The music was stilled, the plays ceased, and the artists apparently stopped working as well. Paintings and drawings, however, have a life of their own, and many of them miraculously survived. Dozens of them are safeguarded at the Art Museum of Yad Vashem, testimony to the victory of the spirit.

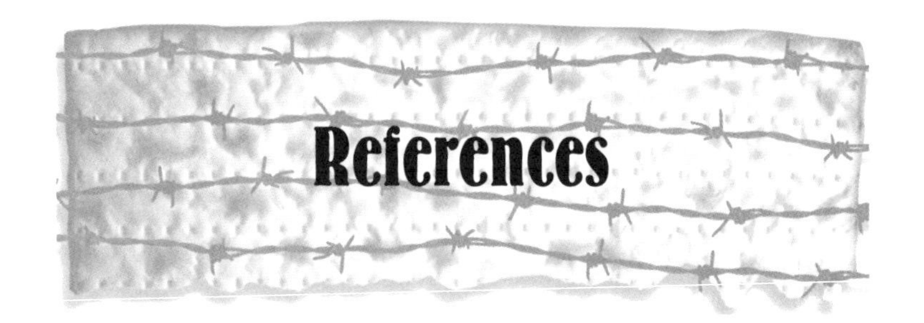

Hovav, Meir. *"Al Haggadat Mahane Gurs She-B'Tzarfat"* (About the Haggadah of Gurs, France), *HaTzofeh*, 14 *Nissan* 5744.

Yodlov, Yitzhak. *"Otzar HaHagadot – Bibliographia Shel Haggadot Pesah MeReishit HaDfus Ha'Ivri Ad Shnat T'Sh'Kh"* (A Treasury of Haggadot A Bibliography of Passover Haggadot from the Beginning of Hebrew Printing Until 5720), *Mifal HaBibliographia Ha'Ivrit* (The Hebrew Bibliography Project). Magnes Press, 5757.

Ya'ari, Avraham. *"Bibliographia Shel Haggadot Pesah MeReishit HaDfus Ve'Ad Hayom"* (A Bibliography of Passover Haggadot from the Beginning of Printing Until Today). Bamberger and Wahrman, 5721.

Morgenstern, Naomi. *"BaMistor"* (In Hiding), *Yeladim BeTkufat HaSho'ah BeTzarfat* (Children During the Holocaust Period in France). The International School for Holocaust Studies, Yad Vashem, 5758.

Neter, Yitzhak Eugen. *"Sabba Neter"* (Grandpa Neter): *Tishrei* 5637-24 *Tishrei* 5727. Degania Aleph 1986.

"Edut Tziyurim Min HaSho'ah" (Testimony Pictures from the Holocaust). Yad Vashem Art Museum, 5742.

Poznanski, Renée. *"Beshvil HaZikaron, HaHa'im BeMahanot HaYehudim Bedrom Tzarfat, 1940-1942"* (For Memory's Sake, Life in the Jewish Camps in Southern France, 1940-1942). The International School for Holocaust Studies, Yad Vashem.

Poznanski, Renée. *"LeHiyot Yehudi BeTzarfat 1939-1945"* (To Be a Jew in France 1939-1945). Yad Vashem, 5760.

Frankl, Viktor. *"Ha'Adam Mehapes Mashma'ut"* (Man's Search for Meaning). Dvir, 5733.

Kappel, Shmu'el René. *"Ma'avak Yehudi BeTzarfat HaKevusha BaMahanot HaHesger U-Va'irgun HaYehudi HaLohem (1940-1944)"* (The Jewish Struggle in Occupied France in the Detention Camps and in the Jewish Fighters' Organization [1940-1944]). Yad Vashem.

Kremer, Yitzhak. *"BeMazal U'VeTevunah"* (With Luck and with Understanding). Moreshet, 5760.

Shteindling, Dolly. *"'Vina, Tzarfat, Vina,' Korotav shel Palit VeLohem Mahteret Yehudi"* ('Vienna, France, Vienna,' The Story of a Jewish Refugee and Underground Fighter). Jerusalem.

Yad Vashem Archives. Oral and Written Testimonies of Rabbi Yehudah Ansbacher, Pinhas Rothschild, Rafi Flatto, Binyamin Zomer, Ehud Loeb.

Barosin, Jacob
Born in Russia and immigrated with his parents to Germany; studied painting in the Academy of Art in Berlin; doctorate in Art History from the University of Freiburg. Immigrated to Paris with the Nazis' rise to power in 1933. Wandered in southern France for an extended time. In the spring of 1943, he was imprisoned at Gurs, from which he escaped after several months. Assisted by local Catholics, he hid in several places in southern France but was forced to return to Paris where he hid until its liberation. In 1947, he immigrated to the United States.

Berkefeld, Harry
Born in 1898. Arrived at Gurs from Brems in March 1941. Left Gurs with the assistance of the Foreign Legion, a work force set up by the Vichy government as national service. As far as is known, he illustrated the diary of Theodore Rosenthal about life at the Gurs camp.

Bodek, Karl
Born in Czechoslovakia in 1905. Arrested and sent to the Saint Cyprien camp in October 1940 and then to the Gurs camp. Worked together with the artist Kurt Loew. He was also active in cabaret scenery design and painted the prisoner "stamps" in which he protested the deplorable conditions at the Gurs camp. In 1941 he was transferred to the Les Milles camp and from there, after failing in all his attempts to escape, was put on the transport to the death camps.

Breuer, Leo
Born in Bonn in 1893. Officially listed as Catholic and Jewish. Studied art in Cologne, fought in World War I and was captured in the USSR. He continued his studies after the war in Cologne and in Kassel. Lived in Berlin and in Holland during 1930-1934 and moved to Belgium in 1935. He was a painter and also designed and exhibited scenery. He was imprisoned in 1940 and sent to the Saint Cyprien camp. In October of that same year he was transferred to the Gurs camp, where he worked as a Catholic Relief Agency worker. He was a prolific artist at the camp and many of his pictures have been preserved. He left the camp in October 1943 for the Chateau de Chancy at Rouen. After the war he settled in Paris.

Hofstatter, Osias
Born in Poland in 1905. Lived in Vienna from 1921 to 1938. In 1938, with the fall of Austria, he fled to Luxembourg from where he was sent to the Saint Cyprien camp in May 1940. In October of that year he was transferred to the Gurs camp. He started painting while imprisoned at the camp during 1940-1941 until his escape to Switzerland in 1942. He returned to Warsaw after the war in 1948, where he taught in a Jewish orphanage. In 1957 he immigrated to Israel, and only in the 1970s did his extensive artistic career begin. Many of the paintings from the camp, which he succeeded in smuggling into Switzerland, are in the collections at the Ghetto Fighters House and the Museum at Yad Vashem. Hofstatter died in 1994 in Tel Aviv.

Loew, Kurt (Conrad)
Born in Vienna in 1914, worked as a textile designer while studying at the Academy of Fine Arts in Vienna. He was imprisoned for a short time in 1938 because of his political activity. In 1939 he managed to escape to Belgium where he continued his academic studies in Antwerp. In 1940 he was arrested and sent to the Saint Cyprien camp, and from there to the Gurs camp. While there, together with his friend, the artist Karl Bodek, he utilized his graphic skills to design sets and greeting cards. With the intervention of the International Red Cross in Geneva he was transferred to the Rivesaltes camp; he was liberated in 1942 and returned to Geneva. He held many exhibits in Switzerland until his return to his native Vienna in 1952. He died in 1980.

Prinz, Kurt
We have no biographical information on this artist, except for the fact that he painted at the Gurs camp.

Schleifer, Fritz
Born in Vienna in 1896. After completing his studies, he moved to Paris. With the outbreak of World War II he was sent to the Gurs camp. He appears on camp lists as Frederick Schleifer, occupation: painter. He was sent to the Drancy camp in August 1942 and from there, in early September, to Auschwitz. He was killed in Auschwitz on 5 October 1942.

Schwesig, Karl
Born in 1898 in Germany. After the first World War he completed his studies at the Academy of Fine Arts in Dusseldorf and in the late 1920s joined the Communist Party in Germany. With the Nazis' rise to power he was imprisoned for sixteen months for his activity in the party. In 1935 he escaped to Belgium, but was arrested in 1940 and imprisoned in the Saint Cyprien camp and then transferred to Gurs and afterwards to Noé. From the camps in southern France he made his way to Paris from where he was sent in a transport to Germany and imprisoned again. He was liberated by the Allies in 1945 and died in 1955 in Dusseldorf.

Sigismond, Kolos Vari
A native of Hungary who immigrated to Paris before the outbreak of the war. With the Nazi occupation of the city, he and his wife were imprisoned in the Gurs camp. He was later smuggled into Switzerland. We have no further details on the artist.